Advance praise for *Teams At Work: 7 Keys to Su*

"Finally there is a book available for team members, not just team leaders. I particularly like the emphasis on shared leadership and the importance of individual teams connecting with the entire organization."

> *Dr. Lana Liberto*
> *Director of Education/Organizational Development*
> *Doylestown Hospital*

"*Teams At Work* is a must for educators responsible for the development of teams. By identifying seven elements of successful teams and demonstrating how to implement each element practically, Dr. Zoglio has created an invaluable staff development resource!"

> *Susan W. Sinkinson*
> *Staff Development Facilitator*
> *North Penn School District*

"Suzanne Zoglio's seven keys to success can be applied to any endeavor that requires strong team work. Theatre is a collaboration; each artist has a piece of the garden, but it is the joining of talents, the commitment, and the contributions that create a successful and powerful production."

> *Peter A. Ratray*
> *Associate Director*
> *Mint Theatre, New York City*

TEAMS AT WORK

7 KEYS TO SUCCESS

Suzanne Willis Zoglio

TOWER HILL PRESS   Sky Run Business Center
P.O. Box 1132, Doylestown, PA 18901

Copy editor: Susan Kidney
Proofreader: Alice Lawler
Text/Jacket design: Hilt and Associates, Philadelphia, PA
Typesetting: Hilt and Associates, Philadelphia, PA
Typeface: Goudy

ISBN 0-941668-04-5
Library of Congress Catalog Card No. 93-94078

Printed in the United States of America

To Evelyn Higgins Willis,
who inspired courage and encouraged change.

7 KEYS TO TEAM SUCCESS

1 Commitment

2 Contribution

3 Communication

4 Cooperation

5 Conflict Management

6 Change Management

7 Connections

AUTHOR'S NOTE

As an organizational consultant, I have assisted with the start-up and development of many work teams. Those experiences have strengthened two of my core beliefs related to behavioral change: a) if you want change on the front line, train the front line, not just management, and b) if you want people to change their behaviors, provide operational guidelines, not just theory. This book is a manifestation of those beliefs.

The content of *Teams At Work* is organized around seven key elements of effective teams. It provides managers, trainers, and team leaders with a model for systematically diagnosing and strengthening a team. Perhaps more importantly, this book provides tools for those who participate on work teams. The focus is not on how to lead or manage teams, but on how to be a better team. In addition, while this book is grounded in theory, it is a hands-on guide that offers practical suggestions and structured activities for individuals and teams who want to enhance their effectiveness. My hope is that it will be used, not just read. The ideas offered are straightforward and practical. The activities are easy to implement. The individual exercises are an invitation to each team member to get involved, demonstrate initiative, and turn ideas into action. I hope they serve as a springboard for personal input. All that white space in the margins is included for just that reason...to become a repository of ideas, assessments, and personal "ah-hahs." If that happens, each reader will become a coauthor, turning useful ideas and helpful tools into a personalized resource guide for enhancing teams at work.

Let me share with you my vision for *Teams At Work*. In my consulting with corporations, schools, hospitals, and government agencies, I stumble upon copies everywhere. Some are stacked on trainers' desks; some are peeking out of briefcases; some are perched on top of machines out in the plant; some are comfortably cluttered on conference tables. I even find one next to a vending machine in the cafeteria. They are all marked up, highlighted, and dog-eared from hours of use. I love that image.

Suzanne Willis Zoglio
Bucks County, PA
April 29, 1993

ACKNOWLEDGMENTS

Many clients, friends, family members, and colleagues have supported the development of *Teams At Work*. All of their efforts have been most appreciated. I am especially grateful to the following individuals who so generously gave of their time and talent to critique early drafts and to provide numerous and valuable suggestions: Paul Bolognone (Rohm & Haas DVI), Margery Brodhead (American Express Travel Related Services Company), Steven Horner (Harleysville Insurance Companies), Dr. Lana Liberto (Doylestown Hospital), Dr. Melanie Maloney (SmithKline Beecham), Lou Manzi (SmithKline Beecham), Dawn Robertson (Aetna Life and Casualty), and Susan Sinkinson (North Penn School District).

My editor and designer, Susan Kidney (Hilt and Associates), provided a critical eye, creative support, and numerous enhancing ideas. I truly appreciate the commitment she made to this project and the patience she demonstrated through the many revisions.

Marti Neiman typed and retyped, and regularly cheered me on with her enthusiasm and confidence in the project. Alice Lawler provided not only a professional reader's view, but also generous support.

Most of all, I am grateful to my husband Mike. His relentless urging moved me to action, and his unwavering support saw me through.

INTRODUCTION

As quality, customer service, employee empowerment, and streamlined operations have become benchmarks of good business, so, too, have work teams. Complex organizations responding to complex economic conditions require commitment, communication, and cooperation from employees who bond together to produce results greater than any one individual could achieve. Teams are here to stay, and effective teams are worth the time and energy they take to develop.

Each chapter of *Teams At Work* focuses on one of seven key elements of effective teams and explores why it is needed, how to recognize it, what an individual can do to enhance the element, and what a team can do. All of the activities in this book are available as reproducible masters in *50 Activities For Teams At Work* available from Tower Hill Press.

This book will be of interest to team members, team leaders/facilitators, trainers, and managers. Each might use *Teams At Work* a little differently.

HOW TO USE THIS BOOK
Team Members
If you are a member of a work team, use this book to assess and strengthen your personal influence on your team's performance. The worksheets, assessments, and activities will guide your thinking about how you presently contribute to the team. They will support you in becoming an even more positive force. You might use the text as an individualized learning program—completing one chapter at a time, allowing time between chapters to practice what you learned. Or you may wish to suggest that your whole team read the book together and discuss major points at team meetings. Select activities which are especially relevant for your group or simply work your way through the book from beginning to end.

Team Leaders/Facilitators

If you are a leader of a work team, you have probably wondered how to boost the collective power of your group. The seven-keys model provides a road map for doing just that. You can use the book to assess the relative strengths and weaknesses of your team and use the team activities to help you manage improvement. You can use the activities at team meetings or "bundle" them into an off-site retreat. Later you can give the book to each new member who joins your team, as a process orientation manual that provides an overview of what makes an effective team and how individual team members can influence that effectiveness.

Trainers

If you are a trainer charged with enhancing teamwork, you can distribute this book as a support tool to individuals who are about to join an intact team, or provide it as a resource for each member of a self-directed team. You might also use this book as a start-up guide for new task forces or as the foundation for a basic course on how to work effectively in groups. Or you can give it to managers who ask for help in supporting a new or struggling work team. If you decide to design a course around the book, an accompanying *Leader's Guide* that includes nine lesson plans, *50 Activities For Teams At Work*, and text for overhead transparencies is available.

Managers

Managers are often responsible for overseeing the start-up or development of work teams, but rarely are they told how to help the team. This book provides a good model—the seven keys—to use in designing, developing, or evaluating a team. It also provides numerous ideas for enhancing each essential element. It will prepare you to effectively coach a team and will provide a handy reference when a team leader comes to you for help. It will also help you to be a better contributor to your own management team.

SEVEN KEYS TO TEAM SUCCESS

While there are many factors that contribute to the effectiveness of a work team, high-performance teams share certain traits. These traits have been researched in the literature repeatedly and listed under a variety of terms. The seven elements discussed in this book are consistent with research findings on team effectiveness but hopefully provide a fresh perspective and a "user friendly" model. One element that is given less emphasis here than in the literature is leadership. Since there are many books on formal leadership, the emphasis in this book is on shared, rotational leadership, and is discussed in relation to team member contribution.

Consulting with various types of work groups over the years—task forces, self-directed teams, departments, business units—I have observed how important it is for teams to develop strong individual contribution and shared commitment to goals, as well as advanced skills in effective communication, workplace cooperation, and conflict management. In addition, if high-performance teams are going to add to organizational success, they must learn to welcome change and make positive connections. Each chapter of *Teams At Work* focuses on one of these seven elements and explores why it is needed, how to recognize it, what an individual can do to enhance it, and what a team can do to enhance it.

CONTENTS

1 **COMMITMENT** • 1
What can you do to enhance commitment? • 5
What can your team do to enhance commitment? • 10
Summary • 19

2 **CONTRIBUTION** • 21
What can you do to enhance contribution? • 24
What can your team do to enhance contribution? • 30
Summary • 34

3 **COMMUNICATION** • 35
What can you do to enhance communication? • 39
What can your team do to enhance communication? • 45
Summary • 50

4 **COOPERATION** • 51
What can you do to enhance cooperation? • 57
What can your team do to enhance cooperation? • 60
Summary • 66

5 **CONFLICT MANAGEMENT** • 67
What can you do to enhance conflict management? • 70
What can your team do to enhance conflict management? • 78
Summary • 83

6 **CHANGE MANAGEMENT** • 85
What can you do to enhance change management? • 88
What can your team do to enhance change management? • 99
Summary • 106

7 **CONNECTIONS** • 107
What can you do to enhance connections? • 110
What can your team do to enhance connections? • 116
Summary • 121

"It is not enough to be busy… the question is: 'What are we busy about?'"

Henry David Thoreau

COMMITMENT

NOTES

A work team, like a winning sports team, needs to agree on its mission, values, and goals for achieving success. Team members must be willing to put aside their own personal goals for the good of the team. Otherwise, the result is a collective of great performers, not a team. Imagine five basketball players who each decide to follow their personal instincts about winning the game. One player might decide to emphasize defense, another offense; one might experiment with new plays, another might stick to old standards. Chaos would reign.

With a clarity of purpose and values that are aligned with the organization, a team can visualize its connection to organizational success, see its role in the big picture, and realize that it has the power to influence something bigger than itself. Only then does a team really commit to performance goals and measurable objectives. When members make such a commitment to move toward the same goal, energy is directed and the group creates a synergy—a force greater than the combined energy of its individual members. Strong team commitment holds groups together and allows them to stretch for collective excellence. With commitment, everyone seems to be heading down the same track to an agreed-upon destination.

How to Recognize Strong Commitment

When a work group develops a high level of commitment among its members, several things become apparent. Members are able to articulate the team's purpose and how its performance affects the success of the larger organization; that is, they can describe what they do and why their work is important. Also, they can list the important values which guide their decisions and translate those values into everyday behaviors or practices. Team members are focused on specific goals, know what measures indicate success, and, when they hit their targets, celebrate as a team.

To commit to a team, members need to know how team performance impacts the larger organization.

One way to assess a team's level of commitment is to assess the clarity of a team's mission and values. Ask group members to describe why the team exists—its real purpose. For instance, suppose you were to ask a hospital emergency room nurse about the purpose of his department and he answered, "Well, basically, we're here to save lives. We hope to do that by providing the best medical care as quickly as possible, while making the patient as comfortable as possible."

Would that response indicate a clear understanding of purpose? Probably, since most of us would agree that the primary purpose of a hospital emergency room is to provide the best medical care as quickly as possible, while keeping the patient comfortable. The nurse's response would not only demonstrate a clear understanding of team purpose, but also of core team values—care, speed, and comfort—all critical to emergency room success.

Contrast the nurse's response with this example:

You request a paper cup from a young restaurant clerk so that you can take your coffee with you. She answers, "I'm sorry. I can't give you a take-out cup. You'll have to go to the take-out window." After a brief exchange, you ask her what she considers to be the most important part of her job. She says, "Well, I don't really know...waiting on the customers, I guess." You can't help thinking that although the young woman is not slow or discourteous, she is also not committed to a vision (e.g., satisfying the customer) or any guiding principles (e.g., doing whatever it takes). For the young waitress it seems that commitment to waiting on the customer is not a commitment to service excellence. Yet, in the restaurant lobby, a framed service statement reads, "Our Commitment: Satisfy the Customer...Whatever It Takes."

Another way to assess level of commitment is to assess clarity of team goals and objectives. When asked how his team's mission translated into specific goals, suppose the nurse mentioned earlier answered without any hesitation, "We need to follow treatment protocol, reduce average patient wait time, eliminate X-ray retakes, and improve patient satisfaction." That response would indicate that a picture of success was broken down into performance priorities which directed day-to-day work behaviors. Contrast that response with this example:

A manufacturing company recently committed to increasing the involvement of its employees in the management and operations of the plant. Although the company had embarked on a job redesign project in which the workers were trained in team processes such as

Commitment is more than a motto... commitment means "walking the talk."

Improvement TIP

group decision making, shared leadership, and meeting management, employees were unclear about priority goals. When asked what their performance objectives were, none could answer, except in very general terms. One individual said that improving productivity was a group objective, although she had no idea how it would be measured. Another said that keeping the customer satisfied was a priority, although he did not really know how satisfied customers were at the present time. A third indicated that improving safety in the plant was important, although she didn't know why, since she knew of no safety problems.

When team commitment is high, goals and measures are not vague. Members can readily explain how purpose translates into priority goals, specific objectives, and performance measures.

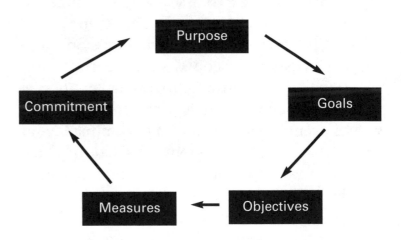

What Can You Do To Enhance Commitment?

3 INDIVIDUAL
IMPROVEMENT
STRATEGIES

1. Focus on team purpose and values.

2. Clarify your own purpose and values.

3. Consider how your purpose and values fit with your team's.

Focus on Team Purpose and Values

To be effective as a team member, you need to be clear about your team's basic purpose...its mission. As Stephen Covey discusses in *Seven Habits of Highly Effective People*, it is important to "begin with the end in mind." In a sentence or two you should be able to clearly state why your team exists and what organizational values guide decision making in your group. Whether you are a member of a task force, a department, or an intact production team, your commitment will be higher if you know your team's primary purpose, how that purpose impacts your organization's success, and how it fits with your personal vision of success.

To determine how well you understand your group's purpose, briefly try to describe why your team exists. Then list the core values for your team. If you have difficulty doing so, ask to discuss your team's mission and values at your next team meeting. If the group also has difficulty describing its shared mission and important values, arrange for a facilitator to conduct a meeting where you can clarify both as a group.

Improvement
TIP

Team Purpose and Values

1. Briefly describe (in a sentence or two) your organization's primary purpose. Why does the organization exist?

2. Briefly describe (in a sentence or two) your team's primary purpose. Why does your team exist?

3. List three to seven values that are important to your organization and your team (e.g., to be of service to others, to show respect to coworkers, to be creative, to have fun, to be frugal, to collaborate, to be honest).

   •

   •

   •

   •

   •

   •

   •

Clarify Your Own Purpose and Values

Even if you have not given much thought to your primary purpose in life or to your personal values, you may have given thought to what kind of person you hope to become and what you hope to accomplish before you die. Perhaps you have visualized what success means to you. For many people the ultimate success is achieving their goals while living by their own standards or values. Unfortunately, many individuals speak of empty successes because they achieved goals but did not live by values that were important to them.

If your own purpose and values are compatible with those of your work team it is more likely that you will be committed to your team's priorities. But before you can address the issue of compatibility, you will need to do a little soul searching.

> **THREE ELEMENTS OF PURPOSE**
> - accomplishments
> - role performance
> - values

My Purpose and Values Statement

One way to clarify purpose is to focus on what you hope to accomplish, how you hope to lead your various life roles, and which values you hope are reflected in your life.

1. List the major things you hope to accomplish before you die (e.g., develop a business, write a book, teach people to teach better).

2. What roles are most important to you and how would you like to handle them (e.g., parent you can count on, loyal friend, boss that develops others, sibling who stays in touch)?

3. What values do you want others to associate with you (e.g., integrity, pursuit of excellence, humor, patience, risk taking, flexibility)?

Consider How Your Purpose and Values Fit With Your Team's

If you don't believe in your team's purpose, you can't commit to the team.

If your team's purpose is compatible with your own purpose, you are more likely to feel in step with your group. If not, you may feel pulled in two directions. It is important, therefore, to analyze how worthwhile you find your team's purpose. Is it a purpose you can believe in? Is it aligned with your personal mission? Do team values fit with your personal values? If there is not a perfect fit, you may be able to create ways of satisfying both. For example, if you really value direct communication, and your team places a strong value on peace and harmony, you might feel like a fish out of water much of the time. But you could resolve such conflict by learning to be more tactful in your verbal exchanges, which would preserve both harmony and honesty. You could also ask your team to support your value of honesty by adopting a few ground rules about disagreeing agreeably.

Before you can address any differences, however, you will need to identify them.

Checking the Fit Between Individual/Team Purpose

1. To what extent is your team's purpose compatible with your own purpose?

2. Which of your strong personal values are also important to your team (e.g., honesty, hard work, creativity, helpfulness)?

3. Do any team values conflict with your personal values? (e.g., you value honesty; your team values harmony... You value independence; your team values group input on everything)?

4. Could any conflicts be worked out? How?

What Can Your Team Do To Enhance Commitment?

5 TEAM IMPROVEMENT STRATEGIES

1. Keep the team's mission statement visible.
2.. Develop a shared vision of success.
3. Translate your vision into goals and objectives.
4. Agree on measures of success.
5. Celebrate success milestones.

Keep the Team's Mission Statement Visible

Just as many large organizations develop mission statements which clarify purpose and values, teams should develop their own. While each team's mission should evolve from the larger organization's mission, it should be specific to that team and reflect its unique contribution to the larger organization. In addition, the values reflected in a team statement should be consistent with the organization's stated values and translated into behaviors or practices specific to that team. Once a team mission statement is developed, it should be kept visible and referred to regularly for team direction.

If you do not have a team mission statement, TEAM ACTIVITY 1: CLARIFYING YOUR TEAM'S MISSION*, provides a six-step method you might try.

*Reproducible masters of Team Activity 1 and all other individual and team activities in this book can be found in *50 Activities For Teams At Work*, Suzanne Willis Zoglio, Tower Hill Press, Doylestown, PA.

team activity

1

CLARIFYING YOUR TEAM'S MISSION

Step 1: Each team member takes 5 to 10 minutes to write one sentence which describes the purpose of your team. The sentences might begin with, "We exist in order to..." or "Our team's main purpose is to...."

Step 2: Members work in pairs for 20 to 30 minutes to share their individual sentences and to create one new statement that satisfies both participants.

Step 3: Each pair combines with another pair for 20 to 30 minutes to share their purpose statements and to create one new statement that satisfies all four participants.

Step 4: Post all of the statements generated by the groups of four and discuss as a whole group, highlighting the parts of each statement that everyone agrees on.

Step 5: Create a statement of purpose from the highlighted phrases.

Step 6: With the whole team, review the core organizational values and brainstorm team practices that reflect those values.

You now have the basis (purpose and values) of a team mission statement.

Develop a Shared Vision of Success

If you have a team leader or a trained group facilitator, ask one to lead your group in a visioning exercise. This activity should include discussing your team's vision of success (the broad picture of what you'd like the team to look like in two or three years) based on your purpose and core values.

Improvement
TIP

If you do not have a trained facilitator available, try following the steps outlined in TEAM ACTIVITY 2: DEVELOPING A SHARED VISION OF SUCCESS.

2 DEVELOPING A SHARED VISION OF SUCCESS

Complete each step below.

Step 1: Individual members jot down what they hope the team will be like in two to three years. Consider at least these elements:
- service/product quality
- image within constituency
- value to organization
- team work climate

Step 2: Work in small groups to share individual visions, discuss commonalities, and create a joint vision. Each group should think metaphorically about the ideal team (e.g., We are a silver bullet: brilliant, strong, fast, powerful) or to draw a picture of their ideal team (e.g., a wheel with a hub and strong spokes).

Step 3: Each subgroup reports to the large group. Highlight the elements common to each group.

Step 4: Using the highlighted elements, create together one clear vision of your future team.

Translate Your Vision Into Goals and Objectives

Translating generalities into specifics is not easy, but it is essential for enhancing commitment to a team and ensuring that everyone is on the same track. Consider this example:

As part of its vision statement, a travel agency states that it wants to become the agency of choice for most corporate clients in the area.

Suppose you were a travel agent with that organization—how would you determine how to increase success? Increase the number of new corporate clients? Increase the satisfaction of old clients? How would you work toward that goal on a day-to-day basis? And how would you support team members to achieve the group vision?

It is important to translate your group's vision into a few priorities and then to translate those priority goals into specific, measurable objectives. To enhance commitment in your work group, focus on a few priority goals and list specific objectives that will help you achieve each goal. TEAM ACTIVITY 3: TRANSLATING TEAM VISION INTO GOALS, illustrates how to accomplish this.

Commitment means "walking the talk." And this is where many work groups fall flat on their collective faces. They verbally commit to a

Improvement
TIP

---

team activity

3 TRANSLATING TEAM VISION INTO GOALS

Step 1: List three to four priority goals related to your group's vision. Listing your goals will get everyone going in the same direction. Use the boxes provided. (*Examples: Improve customer satisfaction, increase productivity, enhance work safety, empower employees*).

Step 2: Develop two to three specific objectives for each goal listed by answering the question, "How will we know when we have made progress toward our goals?" Developing objectives will ensure that everyone in your group is on the same track.

Example:

GOAL: Improve Customer Satisfaction

OBJ A. Reduce service turnaround time

OBJ B. Increase number of special requests filled

OBJ C. Improve service ratings

GOAL 1:

OBJ A:

OBJ B:

OBJ C:

Team Activity 3 continues...

shared vision, but they don't know how that commitment really affects everyday work behaviors. Here is a case that illustrates the point:

A marketing group from a pharmaceutical company developed a vision that included a "collaborative work environment." That sounds simple and sensible, doesn't it? People working together for the good of the department. However, this group did not agree on what behaviors constitute collaboration. Each team member left the visioning meeting expecting different collaborative behaviors. So, three weeks later, team members began grumbling that some people were not honoring the group's commitment to collaborative behavior. Complaints ranged from, "People are not answering phone calls promptly," and "We're not sharing client information," to "Only a few are attending our Friday lunch meetings."

Perceptions differ; therefore, principles and values should be discussed in terms of practices.

Do these comments indicate that those individuals were not committed to collaborating with their colleagues? No, but they do indicate differences in perceptions of what constitutes collaboration. General commitment to an ideal is not enough to move the team forward; a team needs commitment to specific behaviors. The pharmaceutical marketing group might have discussed whether sharing information, attending each other's presentations, and celebrating each other's successes constituted collaborative behaviors. With such specific behaviors in mind, each member would have been able to commit to increasing those behaviors. Also, the group would have been able to measure frequency of these behaviors, indicating whether collaboration was going up or down.

As a group moves from agreement on principles to identification of specific practices that embody those principles, commitment climbs.

Agree on Measures of Success

Once your team has clarified its vision and developed related goals and objectives, it is important to measure team success and conduct regular performance feedback sessions to clarify just how much progress is being made toward group goals. Individuals need to know the impact of their efforts if they are going to continue investing energy. Since feedback on performance is both motivating and directing, it not only sparks energy for change, but also focuses that energy on which improvement areas are most likely to yield a good return.

As a work group, you need to determine what information will tell you if you are on the right track or if you need to move in another direction. For example, if improving customer service is a goal for your group, consider these sources of information as measures of your success:

- Results of a customer feedback survey
- Number of word-of-mouth referrals
- Project turnaround time
- Comments from customer focus groups

If you are not sure which measures will indicate how well your group is doing, try to identify measures at your next team meeting. Perhaps as a team you could complete an activity similar to that described in TEAM ACTIVITY 4: MEASURING TEAM SUCCESS. Remember to consider information that is already being collected as well as new data you might collect. When you have a good listing of possible measures, review the list. See if any measures duplicate one another or are too costly or time consuming to implement.

What gets measured, gets done.

PERFORMANCE FEEDBACK IS
- **motivating**
- **directing**

Improvement
TIP

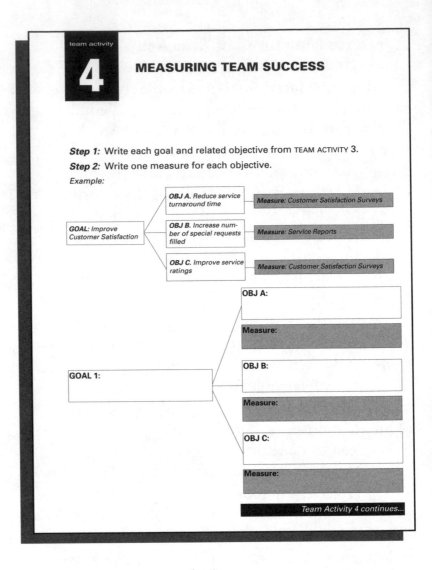

team activity

4 MEASURING TEAM SUCCESS

Step 1: Write each goal and related objective from TEAM ACTIVITY 3.

Step 2: Write one measure for each objective.

Example:

GOAL: Improve Customer Satisfaction

OBJ A. Reduce service turnaround time — **Measure:** Customer Satisfaction Surveys

OBJ B. Increase number of special requests filled — **Measure:** Service Reports

OBJ C. Improve service ratings — **Measure:** Customer Satisfaction Surveys

GOAL 1:

OBJ A:

Measure:

OBJ B:

Measure:

OBJ C:

Measure:

Team Activity 4 continues...

Improvement **TIP**

As a group, before you agree to start using any measures, explore how you will handle the information. How will you collect the data? How will you analyze it? How will your group use the information? It is also wise to do some responsibility charting. Who will be responsible for tracking the data? Who will develop related graphs? Who will set up any computer databases?

Celebrate Success Milestones

Celebrating team successes, no matter how small, is important to building commitment because it enhances confidence in team goals and provides evidence that efforts are paying off. If celebrations of success are too far apart, team members will begin to wonder if the goal is achievable at all. No one is motivated to work toward unattainable goals. Most of us need to see that we are making progress, that our efforts are paying off and that continued commitment will result in success. Individuals are most motivated when they believe two things: that they can succeed, and that such success will result in a valued reward.

Celebrations may serve as rewards in and of themselves (e.g., camaraderie, self-pride, peer recognition), or indicate possible future rewards (e.g., promotion, job security, more influence). In any case, celebrations are always important to group commitment.

If your work team does not celebrate often, it is possible that your colleagues do not see the value in celebrations. Perhaps you could bring up the importance of milestone celebrations at a future team meeting. Be sure to share your thoughts on which milestones would make good celebration points.

For instance, if you are working toward productivity improvement, you might celebrate when you reach a 10% improvement level. If you are concerned with customer service, you might celebrate the first 95% positive response rate. If improved methods are important, you might celebrate when your last team member completes an important skills course. Discuss team goals, determine appropriate milestones, and then celebrate.

TWO BELIEFS THAT MOTIVATE
- **success is possible**
- **success will be rewarded**

Improvement
TIP

Consider a few of these ideas for acknowledging accomplishments and celebrating team success:

- Pizza party at work
- Cake (decorated for the related success)
- Hand-painted balloon for each member
- "We did it!" buttons, mugs, etc.
- Congratulations announcements on bulletin boards
- Banners in the work area

To brainstorm more ideas, discuss celebrations at a team meeting, addressing questions similar to those found in TEAM ACTIVITY 5: YOUR TEAM'S WAY OF CELEBRATING.

---

team activity

5   YOUR TEAM'S WAY OF CELEBRATING

1. What are likely milestones (small successes) toward your big goals?

2. What celebration activities do you all enjoy?

3. Should you avoid any types of celebrations (e.g., offensive to some, too expensive, too time consuming, or poor public relations)?

4. How might you match the celebration to the milestone (e.g., blowout for bigger achievements, donuts for smaller ones)?

CHAPTER 1
SUMMARY

- When team commitment is high, work groups are more productive and enjoy a more satisfying work environment.

- A team's purpose and values should fit with the organization's purpose and values.

- Teams need members who will commit to a shared purpose and values and will put team goals before personal needs.

- Members can enhance commitment by focusing on team purpose and values and by considering how their own purpose and values fit with the team's.

- Teams can enhance commitment by keeping the team's mission visible, developing a shared vision of success, formulating priority goals, measuring success, and celebrating together.

"Feelings about membership, control, and skills influence our motivation, which in turn, determines the quality of our own work."

Marvin R. Weisbord
Productive Workplaces

CONTRIBUTION

NOTES

The power of an effective work team is in direct proportion to the skills its members possess and the initiative its members expend. Teams need members who have strong skills and who are willing to continually develop new skills. Teams also need self-leaders who do what it takes without being told, and informal leaders who step forward to take charge when it is appropriate.

    With balanced contribution a team can tap the wide range of ideas and talent present in a group and protect itself from member burnout. If the same few people do most of the work, initiate most of the ideas, and assume most of the leadership, a team risks member turnover or an even more threatening condition—member turnoff. To avoid these conditions and to keep energy flowing, each member has to take a turn at bat...every game, every season, every year. The level of team contribution is affected by three factors worth exploring: how included members feel, how confident members feel, and how empowered members feel.

Improvement
TIP

**MEMBERS FEEL
INCLUDED WHEN**

- they are kept
  informed

- their input is
  solicited

The more team members feel like part of the team, the more they contribute; the more they contribute, the more they feel like part of the team. Individuals contribute significantly more to a team when they feel included. To increase feelings of belonging, teams need to keep all members informed, solicit input from everyone, and increase an atmosphere of collegiality.

To contribute in a meaningful way, team members need to feel confident as well as included. They must believe that they have the skills and the necessary resources to succeed. Diversity on a team often means that some individuals may be well trained in technical areas, but sorely unprepared to lead a group meeting. Others may be quite proficient in group processes, but know little about training a new recruit. Therefore, for maximum effectiveness, a team must initially match talent to the task and continually develop team talent for confident performance.

**For contribution to
occur, members must
believe in themselves
and believe in the team.**

Confidence in the team also impacts a member's contribution level. If members are not sure that their investment of time and energy will really make a difference, they are less willing to take additional training, volunteer as rotational leaders, accept extra assignments, or pinch hit for others. For enhanced contribution, members must believe in the collective talent of the team and in the probability of its success.

**TO FEEL EMPOWERED,
MEMBERS MUST**

- participate in
  decisions

- be given tools

- be respected for
  experience

Empowerment also impacts contribution. When individuals participate in decisions that affect them, they are more likely to contribute significantly to the group. As team members are given the tools and authority necessary to do a good job, they become more interested in the success of the group. To be asked for ideas, be included in decision making, and be respected for experience adds a good deal to the quality of work life. The enhanced sense of control increases motivation to contribute.

How to Recognize Strong Team Contribution

Meeting attendance is usually better when contribution to the group is high, because contributing individuals feel important and needed; they realize their presence at meetings is appreciated.

Meetings are also more productive; when many members contribute their diverse opinions, innovation and problem solving are enhanced. It might be difficult to recognize an official leader, however, because meeting leadership often rotates when contribution is high. At various times during the meeting, different individuals provide direction, clarification, suggestions for process, and reminders of group goals. There is a comfortable rhythm of leadership as individuals initiate, then follow; follow, then initiate.

When contribution is strong, individuals seem to know what is expected of them. They keep their commitments, volunteer for extra assignments, and frequently enroll in professional development training. A team of strong contributors normally surpasses the objectives it sets.

What Can You Do To Enhance Contribution?

5 INDIVIDUAL IMPROVEMENT STRATEGIES

1. Assess how you contribute.
2. Consider how you support others.
3. Develop confidence in your team.
4. Enhance your own abilities.
5. Focus on the benefits of contribution.

Assess How You Contribute

Before assessing how others contribute to your work team, take stock of your own level of contribution. Consider how often you participate at meetings, volunteer for special assignments, generate new ideas, and generally add value to your team. Try to analyze where you are making a positive contribution to your work team and where you might be able to contribute even more.

Measuring Your Contribution

1. How clear is your role on the team?

   a. very clear   b. clear   c. unclear   d. very unclear

2. How many team meetings have you missed in the last three months?

   a. 0   b. 1   c. 2   d. 3+

3. How many times in the last month have you shared a tip, tool, or resource?

   a. 4+   b. 2–3   c. 1   d. 0

4. How many times in the last six months have you volunteered for a "special assignment"?

   a. 5–6   b. 3–4   c. 2–3   d. 0–1

5. How often in an average month do you suggest new ideas for improving things?

   a. 3   b. 2   c. 1   d. 0

6. How often in an average work day do you offer to help team members, including your team leader, without being asked?

   a. 3   b. 2   c. 1   d. 0

To determine your score, give yourself the following points for each letter you circled: a=3 points, b=2 points, c=1 point, and d=0 points.

Total Score:_____

If your score is less than 12, there is room for improvement. To improve, focus on one behavior for a month. Then focus on improving a second behavior, and so on.

Consider How You Support Others

For an effective team, individuals must be willing to take risks and do what it takes to move the group forward. This willingness to become involved, initiate, and make an extra effort is the soul of an effective work group. It distinguishes talkers from doers, lip service from belief-driven action. Such willingness also requires nurturing and support from colleagues. How well do you encourage others to contribute?

MEMBERS SHOW SUPPORT BY

- listening
- differing with ideas not people
- recognizing others

Encouraging Contribution

1. At meetings, do you listen well to others?

   a. usually   b. frequently c. sometimes d. seldom

2. When you disagree with others, how often do you differ with the idea, not the person, encouraging members to share even unusual ideas or minority opinions?

   a. usually   b. frequently   c. sometimes   d. seldom

3. How often do you recognize special talents of your colleagues by asking them for input on particular projects?

   a. usually   b. frequently   c. sometimes   d. seldom

4. If other members miss a meeting, how often do you let them know that they were missed, perhaps expressing your disappointment because you would have liked their input on something?

   a. usually   b. frequently   c. sometimes   d. seldom

5. How often do you personally compliment team members when they offer ideas, facilitate decision making, or put aside personal interests for the good of the group?

   a. usually   b. frequently   c. sometimes   d. seldom

Develop Confidence in Your Team

Confidence in a team's ability to succeed greatly influences its overall performance. It also influences individual motivation to contribute to the team. How confident are you that your team can successfully accomplish its stated goals? For instance, if you go to meetings, take on leadership assignments, or learn new skills, will your investment make a difference? No one likes wasting time or energy, and most of us invest only when we believe the investment will result in success.

If your confidence in your group is low, think about why you feel that way and what would bolster your confidence. You might try discussing

"This is the power of self-fulfilling prophecy, the Pygmalion effect. People do better if they are expected to do better, and worse if they are expected to do worse."

Robert Waterman
Adhocracy: The Power To Change

your concerns at a team meeting and asking for clarification of specific goals and measures of success. Also, you might focus on team talents, successes, and accomplishments.

Developing Confidence in Your Team

1. What special talents and work experience do your team members have?

2. What successes has the team had in the past year or so?

3. What have individual members accomplished recently?

Enhance Your Own Abilities

If you believe that your group can succeed, do you also believe that you can make a difference? For instance, are you confident that you have the ability to help your group (e.g., act as a rotating leader, represent the group to management, contribute to problem solving, train new members)? If not, you might want to check your assumptions with a few respected members by asking them for feedback on what they see as your strengths and what they see as areas you can develop even more. Identify ways to improve yourself. Wanting to contribute to your group is not enough; you have to continually increase your ability to contribute.

Given the needs of your work group, consider to what extent you are presently able to contribute and to what extent you are willing to become more prepared. Your answers will provide direction for your professional development activities.

Professional Development Plan

1. What technical training would allow you to "pinch hit" for one or more of your colleagues?

2. Since all work groups need meeting facilitators, check which steps you would take to enhance your facilitation skills:

   [ ] read a book

   [ ] take a course

   [ ] co-facilitate a meeting

3. All teams need better group decision-making skills. Are you willing to train with other teams, read books on the subject, or take a seminar?

   [ ] yes   [ ] no

4. What other skills does your group need that you might develop?

Focus on the Benefits of Contribution

If you are confident that your group can succeed and that you can make a strong contribution, the next question is, "Will the end result be personally rewarding?" For instance, if you think that representing your group on a task force will help the team and that you can do a reasonably good job, do you also believe that it will be personally rewarding (e.g., expose you to leadership, create future job contacts, give you higher status on your team)?

To increase your motivation to contribute more, you should be able to answer the question, "What's in it for me"? Know the W.I.I.F.M. and you will increase your motivation. The benefits may be varied: knowing that you have used your talent, being liked and appreciated by team members, or learning something new. Whatever the results, they need to be probable and of value if you are to maintain your motivation. Focus on the rewards of each additional contribution you could make for your group.

The Rewards of Contribution

List three things you could do to increase your contribution to your team. Describe at least one W.I.I.F.M. (personal benefit) of each.

Example:

Contribution	*W.I.I.F.M.*
1. *Learn a new skill*	1. *Increased marketability*
2. *Speak up at meetings*	2. *Respect from team*
3. *Volunteer for task force*	3. *Interesting*

Contribution	W.I.I.F.M.
1.	1.
2.	2.
3.	3.

What Can Your Team Do To Enhance Contribution?

3 TEAM IMPROVEMENT STRATEGIES

1. Measure present contribution.

2. Develop an improvement plan.

3. Reinforce contribution.

*Reproducible masters of Team Activity 6 and all other individual and team activities in this book can be found in *50 Activities For Teams At Work*, Suzanne Willis Zoglio, Tower Hill Press, Doylestown, PA.

Measure Present Contribution

To enhance the contribution level in your group, you need to take the time to measure the present contribution level. Only then can you decide where to direct the group's energy. To determine the contribution level within your work group, start by asking each team member to individually and anonymously evaluate team contribution.

Ask individuals to consider team roles and how well people are suited to their roles. They might also consider two elements of team spirit—willingness to pitch in and enthusiasm at meetings. In addition, members should evaluate individual initiative and confidence in the team. Discuss results at a meeting or ask a neutral party to collect the evaluations and create a group report which reflects the findings but does not identify individual responses.

Discuss the group report at a team meeting. TEAM ACTIVITY 6: TEAM CONTRIBUTION SURVEY*, will give you an idea of what type of questions you might use as a basis for your member survey. Add any questions your group agrees are important to assessing the present level of contribution within your team, and eliminate any questions your team does not find relevant.

In order to take an accurate measure of contributions, make certain that the items you measure are important and that the individuals who evaluate the survey agree to respond honestly.

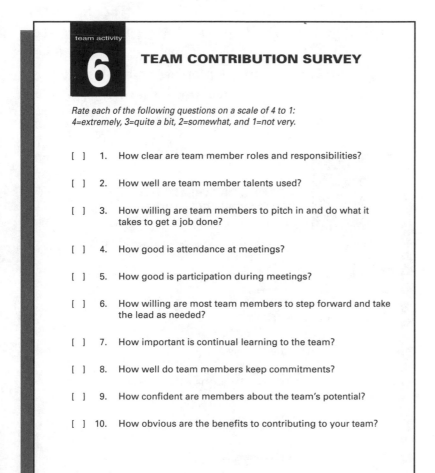

team activity

6

TEAM CONTRIBUTION SURVEY

Rate each of the following questions on a scale of 4 to 1:
4=extremely, 3=quite a bit, 2=somewhat, and 1=not very.

[ ] 1. How clear are team member roles and responsibilities?

[ ] 2. How well are team member talents used?

[ ] 3. How willing are team members to pitch in and do what it takes to get a job done?

[ ] 4. How good is attendance at meetings?

[ ] 5. How good is participation during meetings?

[ ] 6. How willing are most team members to step forward and take the lead as needed?

[ ] 7. How important is continual learning to the team?

[ ] 8. How well do team members keep commitments?

[ ] 9. How confident are members about the team's potential?

[ ] 10. How obvious are the benefits to contributing to your team?

Develop an Improvement Plan

Once you have assessed present strengths and identified areas for improving contribution, your group should discuss the results and develop an action plan. See TEAM ACTIVITY 7: TEAM CONTRIBUTION ENHANCEMENT PLAN for a four-step process. Of course, once you have jointly developed an improvement plan, your team will need to discuss strategies for implementing the plan and monitoring progress.

---

team activity

7 TEAM CONTRIBUTION ENHANCEMENT PLAN

Complete each step below. Refer to the examples presented on back.

Step 1: Identify two to three contribution areas for improvement.
Your improvement area 1:

Your improvement area 2:

Your improvement area 3:

Step 2: For each improvement area, list possible obstacles to improvement.
Obstacles to improvement area 1:

Obstacles to improvement area 2:

Obstacles to improvement area 3:

Step 3: Brainstorm possible actions for improvement.
Your improvement actions for area 1:

Your improvement actions for area 2:

Your improvement actions for area 3:

Step 4: Agree on priorities and recruit a champion for each action. To assist in this important step, you might use a monthly action sheet similar to the example on back.

Team Activity 7 continues...

Reinforce Contribution

While there are many variables which affect how team members contribute to a work group, tendencies of human behavior should be noted. Generally, behavior that is ignored is likely to continue, behavior that is positively reinforced is likely to increase, and behavior that is negatively reinforced is likely to diminish. Therefore, your group has some control over the amount of contribution offered by team members. What you need to consider is which behaviors are being reinforced either positively or negatively.

For example, if a member has not volunteered to be a team facilitator for a long time, is the behavior ignored or discussed? If a team member changes personal travel plans to accommodate scheduling of team training, is it ignored, or do members thank the individual for being a team player? Whatever behaviors your group would like to see increase should be recognized and rewarded. Consider offering something like a "Terrific Teamer" award each month to an individual who has really put team needs first. Or highlight team contributions by creating a "Contributor's Bulletin Board" with photos of top contributors posted each month.

Create ways to positively reinforce the behaviors you want and decide how to confront the behaviors you don't want.

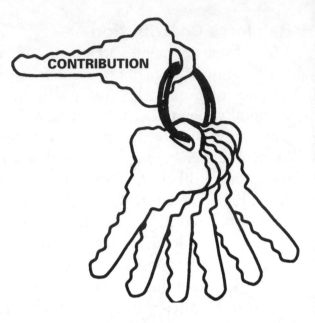

CHAPTER 2
SUMMARY

- Excellent teams need members who will contribute their diverse ideas, unique talents, and varied leadership skills.

- When contribution is high, you will notice more confidence in the group, more individual initiative, better meetings, and improved problem solving.

- Members can enhance contribution by assessing how they personally contribute and support the contribution of others, by developing their own abilities and confidence in the group, and by focusing on the benefits of contribution.

- Teams can enhance contribution by measuring present contribution, developing an improvement plan, and reinforcing high contribution.

"Unprecedented information-sharing, interaction, and recognition are required to induce the attitude change and horizontal communication necessary to foster widespread involvement and commitment."

Tom Peters
Thriving On Chaos

COMMUNICATION

NOTES

For a work group to reach its full potential, members must be able to say what they think, ask for help, share new or unpopular ideas, and risk admitting mistakes. This can only happen in an atmosphere where team members show concern for one another, trust one another, and look for positive solutions, not problems. When communication is friendly, open, and positive, teams are more productive and team members are more satisfied. To achieve such a positive climate team members need to continually enhance their skills in listening, responding, and using language.

Friendly communication results from individuals who know each other, respect each other, and show warmth toward one another. Such behaviors provide an atmosphere for risk taking and cooperation. When team members ask each other about their lives outside of work, respect individual differences, share jokes, and generally make each other feel welcome, they are creating an environment necessary for group cohesiveness.

Open, honest communication is equally important to a team's success. Nothing reduces

Improvement
TIP

trust in a group faster than members saying one thing within the group and something else outside of the group. When members are assertive enough to say what they need to say directly to the appropriate people and to refrain from talking behind each other's backs, trust is enhanced. For a team to adequately assess its performance, members must provide honest feedback, accept objective criticism, and openly review performance measurement data. If members dance around issues, implying but never directly stating what they mean, feedback becomes quite confusing, and performance suffers as a result.

Innovation and continual improvement thrive in an atmosphere which allows honest examination of performance. Team members must trust that mistakes will not be cause for personal attacks. They must believe that although *ideas* may be rejected, *individuals* will never be rejected.

Positive communication impacts the level of motivation and innovation within a work team. When members talk about what they like, want, or need, it is quite different from discussing what they hate or what frustrates them. The former energizes and inspires; the latter drains and demoralizes. Effective teams focus on their dreams rather than their nightmares. They focus on solutions rather than problems and on what they appreciate rather than what they dislike. Positive communication that emphasizes what is right, while directing energy toward making things better, goes a long way in keeping morale high. If members practice the art of reframing—seeing the glass half full instead of half empty—a team greatly increases its chances of becoming a high-performance team. And if members practice the art of solution-sleuthing—looking for answers rather than griping about what's wrong—a team becomes more innovative.

POSITIVE COMMUNICATORS FOCUS ON

• **what they like,** not what they hate

• **what is right,** not what is wrong

• **what they can be,** not what once was

To nurture friendly, open, and positive communication on a team, each member must be skilled in listening, responding, and using language effectively. Since these skills are often taken for granted and assumed to be adequate, a conscious effort is necessary to evaluate each.

While most individuals report that they are good listeners, they rate others as poor listeners. Obviously, someone is not listening well enough. That can block team performance. If people do not hear directions, understand suggestions, or relate to problems, they cannot do the job right. Nor can members perform well if they don't respond to each other or if dialogue is hampered by unclear or uninteresting language. High-performance teams need members with highly developed communication skills.

How to Recognize Strong Communication

If team communication is friendly, open, and positive, team members are skilled in listening, responding, and using language. In an informal, low-tension atmosphere, team members share brief personal exchanges. People speak directly, though tactfully. They listen to each other even though they disagree. While disagreement with ideas is spontaneous, the disagreement is impersonal (e.g., "I wonder if three shifts might complicate communication.") rather than personal (e.g., "Bill, I don't agree with you. Your idea will complicate communication."). There is less beating around the bush, stronger expression of opinions, and lively participation. A definite *can do* atmosphere is prevalent when individuals discuss how to make things better. Although there is appropriate consideration of why things went wrong, the focus is on the solution.

"Listening, really listening, is tough and grinding work, often humbling, sometimes distasteful."

Robert H. Waterman
The Renewal Factor

When communication is strong, meetings are productive, with little grandstanding and few hidden agendas. As members share spontaneously, energy and participation, as well as sincere compliments about individual and group achievements are high. Members frequently check their understanding of what is said and build on each others' ideas—both signs of effective listening. There is less voting and more consensus building reflected in comments such as, "So it seems we can all support plan B, is that right?" The group takes time to consider even far-out ideas. Good-natured humor is apparent at meetings, and members of the team seem to enjoy working with each other.

What Can You Do To Enhance Communication?

3 INDIVIDUAL IMPROVEMENT STRATEGIES

1. Assess your communication style.
2. Set improvement goals.
3. Practice independent learning.

Assess Your Communication Style

To assess your personal communication style, consider how well you listen, respond to others, and use language. Ask a trusted team member for feedback on your communication strengths and weaknesses. You might phrase your request this way:

- In what ways do you think I communicate well?
- What should I work on to become an even better communicator (e.g., being brief, clear, more interesting)?

You might also do some self assessment. Once your assessment is complete, you can establish important communication improvement goals and use independent learning as one way to accomplish them. First, consider how well you listen.

Your Listening Habits

Answer each question below with a *U* for *usually*, O for *occasionally*, or S for *seldom*.

[   ] 1. When others are speaking, do you maintain eye contact?

[   ] 2. When others have spoken, can you repeat the essence of what they said?

[   ] 3. Do you allow speakers to complete their sentences before you comment?

[   ] 4. Do you concentrate fully on what the speaker is saying, instead of on your next comment?

POSITIVE LISTENING HABITS

- maintain eye contact
- repeat the essence
- allow speakers to finish
- focus on content

It is not only important to listen to others, it is also important to let them *know* that you are listening. In other words, to be a good communicator, you have to be a good responder. Your response can communicate attention, empathy, and openness. Check your responding habits.

Your Responding Habits

Answer each question below with a *U* for *usually*, O for *occasionally*, or S for *seldom*.

<table>
<tr><td>

THREE WAYS TO RESPOND

• **reflect feelings**

• **paraphrase**

• **ask questions**

</td></tr>
</table>

[ ] 1. Do you demonstrate that you are listening by reflecting the feeling of the speaker?
Example: "So, you're pretty nervous about the presentation?"

[ ] 2. Do you check your understanding of what others say by paraphrasing the content?
Example: "Your main concern, then, is how to get buy-in from the board?"

[ ] 3. Do you try to expand your understanding of what was said by asking related questions?
Example: "So, we won't save money immediately, but do you believe the new process will save us money in the long run?"

[ ] 4. Do you begin your response with agreement first and objections second?
Example: "I agree that we need to raise prices. I'm concerned about the timing of the increase."

[ ] 5. When disagreeing, do you state under what conditions you could agree?
Example: "I could go along with that idea if we provide training for our associates."

[ ] 6. When disagreeing, do you show respect for the individual's thinking, sharing, and taking a risk?
Example: "That's a creative idea; although it might be too early to try it out , I like the way you keep us on our toes."

To be a good communicator, you not only have to listen and respond appropriately, you also have to use language well. You must be able to express yourself clearly, succinctly, and interestingly. Clarity is enhanced when you choose the right words for a particular audience, know a variety of ways to say the same thing, and have a strong vocabulary. Thinking before you speak also helps you to communicate clearly as you consider what point you wish to make and how best to make it.

Being succinct—a person of few words—is a goal worth working toward. No one likes to call or meet with someone who will predictably ramble on and on. In fact, most of us avoid interactions with such individuals whenever we can, and when we can't, we grit our teeth impatiently. If you are seldom the one to hang up first on the telephone or walk away first from a conversation, you might be too long-winded. If you notice people "glazing over" when you are talking, you could be over-talking. Being succinct is a laudable trait in any work situation, but especially within a team environment. Make it a point to be brief in your comments. Your message will be more powerful and your listeners will be grateful.

Do you know people who have such a way with words that it is a delight to listen to them? Their choice of words, their phrasing, perhaps their witty remarks all manage your attention and keep you interested. Even a person's voice can focus you. Although we can't all have "news broadcaster" voices, we can choose to use language creatively and avoid putting people to sleep. If you have ever suffered through a meeting where one speaker was more boring than the next, you understand. Predictable words, predictable format, humorless content, and monotone delivery all

SKILLFUL SPEAKERS ARE

- clear
- concise
- interesting

MAINTAIN INTEREST WITH

- witty remarks
- anecdotes
- varied tone
- strong vocabulary
- hypothetical questions

encourage mind wandering. To find out how well you maintain interest when you speak, try taping a few of your telephone conversations (your end only) or meeting presentations. Play them back and analyze how interesting you are. Or rate your language skills using the questions below.

Your Language Skills

Answer each question below with a *U* for *usually*, *O* for *occasionally*, or *S* for *seldom*.

[ ] 1. When you have an opinion, can you express it clearly?

[ ] 2. How often do you say things once without others asking you to, "Run that by me again?"

[ ] 3. How often do others say, "I know what you mean?"

[ ] 4. If someone doesn't understand something the first time you say it, do you rephrase your statement on the second try instead of just repeating the same words?

[ ] 5. Do you keep telephone calls brief?

[ ] 6. How frequently are you the party on a call to hang up first?

[ ] 7. When speaking, do you vary your vocabulary?

[ ] 8. When speaking, do you vary your tone?

[ ] 9. When speaking, do you tell interesting stories to illustrate points?

[ ]10. When speaking, do you ask any hypothetical questions to keep your listeners involved?

If you answered *O* or *S* to any of the above questions, put a check (✓) to the left of the question. This indicates a behavior you could work on to improve your language skills.

Set Improvement Goals

Enhancing your communication skills can seem overwhelming. After all, you have been practicing your communication patterns for years. To make the development more manageable, focus on only one improvement area at a time. For example, you might focus on listening more attentively, responding more actively, or being briefer in your comments.

When you decide what behavior you want to work on, set a few related mini-goals. For instance, if your focus is to become a more succinct speaker, you might set a mini-goal of speaking no longer than one minute at a time at your next team meeting. Or you might set a mini-goal of keeping all phone calls one day to three minutes each. Use an egg timer to track your progress. If you succeed with your mini-goal, try it a second time...and a third. Before you know it, the behavior will become a habit, and you will be able to congratulate yourself. In one small step at a time, you can enhance your communication skills. Use mini-goals to focus your improvement energy.

> **"If you don't know where you're going, you'll probably end up somewhere else."**
>
> **Lewis Carroll**
> *Alice In Wonderland*

Communication Mini-Goals

* To listen better, check which improvement action(s) you will try:

[ ] improve eye contact   [ ] take notes while listening

[ ] practice paraphrasing for a day   [ ] rate yourself after each "listen"

[ ] count to three before speaking   [ ] other _____

[ ] remove desk distractions [ ] other _____

- To respond better, check which improvement action(s) you will try:

[ ] use "uh-huh," "I see," nodding   [ ] give compliments on ideas

[ ] don't use "I don't agree"   [ ] use "I could support that if..."

[ ] ask related questions   [ ] other_____

- To use language better, check which improvement action(s) you will try:

[ ] answer all questions with one sentence [ ] use analogies: "It's like..."

[ ] time all telephone calls   [ ] increase voice energy

[ ] hang up first   [ ] other _____

[ ] use anecdotes (stories)   [ ] other _____

Practice Independent Learning

WAYS TO IMPROVE COMMUNICATION SKILLS

- seminars
- reading
- tapes
- modeling

Not all improvement in communication will come from changing habits. Some will come from learning new skills in seminars or workshops. But not all learning takes place in a classroom. There are many ways to enhance your communication skills on your own. You can read articles and books, take a self-study course, listen to self-improvement audio tapes, or watch a video tape development program. You can also model yourself after someone you consider to be a good communicator. Just observe what they do and what they say, and then try out the behaviors yourself. You might also ask someone to act as your coach, giving you specific, targeted feedback on a regular basis.

What Can Your Team Do
To Enhance Communication?

Assess Present Communication Level

To assess the relative strengths and weaknesses of communication within your group, survey each team member individually as in TEAM ACTIVITY 8: TEAM COMMUNICATION SURVEY.* Then discuss strategies for enhancing team communication.

1. Assess present communication level.

2. Schedule team communication training.

3. Monitor team satisfaction with communication.

4. Encourage face-to-face communication.

team activity

8 TEAM COMMUNICATION SURVEY

*Rate each of the following on a scale of 4 to 1 within your group:
4=strongly agree, 3=agree, 2=disagree, 1=strongly disagree.*

[ ] 1. Our group's work goals are clear.

[ ] 2. Our roles in the group are clear.

[ ] 3. We give each other feedback on our performance.

[ ] 4. Team members show respect for each other.

[ ] 5. I frequently hear friendly exchanges between members.

[ ] 6. At meetings there is a high level of participation.

[ ] 7. People generally disagree with ideas, not with individuals.

[ ] 8. Members often give compliments to each other.

[ ] 9. I seldom hear any prolonged griping.

[ ] 10. Members listen to new ideas with an open mind.

[ ] 11. Members are concise when speaking at meetings.

[ ] 12. We generally listen well to each other.

[ ] 13. Individuals generally say what's on their minds.

[ ] 14. Team members do not talk behind each other's backs.

[ ] 15. We are generally "solution-oriented" rather than "problem-petty."

*Reproducible masters of Team Activity 8 and all other individual and team activities in this book can be found in *50 Activities For Teams At Work*, Suzanne Willis Zoglio, Tower Hill Press, Doylestown, PA.

Schedule Team Communication Training

Once you determine what aspects of group communication you would like to improve, you might consider various training opportunities to strengthen those aspects. For instance, if members give compliments very well but do not disagree very well, consider holding a seminar on assertiveness training or asking an internal facilitator to help you establish ground rules for disagreeing agreeably. If your meetings are not as interesting as they might be, consider reading and discussing a self-programmed book on effective meetings, watching an instructional video, or observing another workgroup's meetings. The important thing is to schedule regular training opportunities over a year rather than implementing a one-shot program with no reinforcement.

If you have an in-house training department, ask for help in planning a schedule of learning activities that will move you closer to the type of communication you want to see within your group. If you do not have such support, consider scheduling a formal training program every 10 to 12 weeks and be sure to schedule other activities that reinforce learning (e.g., discuss a magazine article, watch a brief video tape, listen to an audio tape) between programs.

To identify the particular type of communication training that would be most useful for your group, ask team members to rate communication behaviors. TEAM ACTIVITY 9: COMMUNICATION NEEDS ANALYSIS includes a list of team communication behaviors you might want to evaluate.

team activity

9 COMMUNICATION NEEDS ANALYSIS

Rate each item below according to how much training you think your team needs:
3=definite, immediate need; 2=could use improvement; 1=only a brief review
necessary.

[ ]   1.   Saying what we honestly mean.

[ ]   2.   Saying what we mean briefly.

[ ]   3.   Being interesting speakers who hold attention.

[ ]   4.   Listening for facts, details.

[ ]   5.   Listening to a different point of view.

[ ]   6.   Listening when tension is high.

[ ]   7.   Giving each other feedback.

[ ]   8.   Receiving feedback nondefensively.

[ ]   9.   Giving each other compliments.

[ ] 10.   Stating problems positively as questions vs. complaints.

[ ] 11.   Using positive humor.

[ ] 12.   Asking for help.

[ ] 13.   Presenting before groups.

[ ] 14.   Speaking up in meetings.

Monitor Team Satisfaction With Communication

To ensure that communication within your team continues to improve, consider brief monitoring activities on a regular basis. It is much easier to fix communication problems when they are small; taking the pulse of your group regularly increases the probability of success. It also reminds members that communication is important to team effectiveness and is a priority for improvement. TEAM ACTIVITY 10: COMMUNICATION MONITORING TECHNIQUES, provides a few ideas for monitoring how well communications are expanding within your group. Together, your team members can probably generate many more.

team activity

10 COMMUNICATION MONITORING TECHNIQUES

Use the following ideas to enhance communication within your team.

★ At the beginning of a meeting take three minutes to generate a list of adjectives that describe the type of communicators you need for that meeting (e.g., good listeners, open-minded thinkers, concise speakers, tactful dissenters). Keep the list posted in sight as a blueprint for ideal communication.

★ Occasionally, at a break or at the end of the meeting take a written poll of how each member would rate the following: participation, listening, open-mindedness, respect, humor, innovative thinking. Quickly tally the responses on newsprint and take five minutes to brainstorm ways of improving the low areas.

★ Use a "graffiti" sheet in the workplace for members to jot down how they perceive various elements of communication. The heading might read, "This week I'm proud of the way we..." or "We could enhance communication by paying more attention to..." or "I would describe team communication this week as..."

★ Have a feedback "Pollyanna." Each member picks a name of another team member out of a hat and agrees to write that individual a note within the week stating one communication behavior the individual could strengthen and one behavior that is most appreciated. Of course, a personal conference might also be an appropriate follow-up.

Encourage Face-to-Face Communication

Although electronic mail and personal answering machines are great tools, they can be overused. We can become lazy about walking down the hall to see someone and miss out on an informal opportunity for building a stronger relationship. We might send an electronic blurb that will disappear at day's end rather than writing a personal note that would be pinned on a bulletin board or kept in a file. Don't let your team fall victim to electronic depersonalization. Take control and consciously decide the best times and situations for using these important tools. But also encourage regular face-to-face interactions with the team as a whole and among individual members. There is no substitute for a smile, a handshake, or a shared belly laugh.

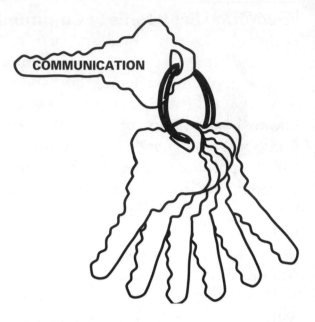

CHAPTER 3
SUMMARY

- Teams need excellent communication to problem-solve effectively, improve work processes, and build a sense of cohesion.

- When communication is high, team members exchange friendly comments, share opinions openly, and talk positively. They listen to each other, respond appropriately, and maintain interest when they speak. Meetings are better, everyone is informed, and the group has more fun.

- Team members can enhance communication by assessing and improving their own style and by encouraging the group to make good communication a priority.

- Teams can enhance communication by assessing present communication, taking training programs, monitoring team satisfaction with communication, and encouraging face-to-face communication.

"Individuals don't win; teams do. Wal-Mart is just a spectacular example of what happens when people find a way to work together…to put their individual egos behind the needs of the team."

Sam Walton
Sam Walton: Made In America

COOPERATION

NOTES

In today's complex world there is only so much any of us can accomplish completely on our own. At work there are few solo opportunities; most challenges require the cooperation of many people. Team members must rely on each other to follow through on assignments, produce quality results, share creative ideas, and contribute to a pleasant work environment. High-performing teams need individuals who are flexible and open-minded enough to make concessions, work for consensus, forgive past mistakes, and contribute to a positive environment.

Cooperation is critical if work teams are to become what innovative corporations of the nineties expect them to be: flexible, efficient, and responsive to customers. To improve processes, quality, and customer satisfaction, colleagues need to share information. To contain costs, they need to share resources. To accommodate continuous training, they need to be flexible, fill in for each other, do whatever it takes—whether it's in their job description or not.

Cooperation is also necessary for high levels of job satisfaction. When there is good cooperation, there is generally more camaraderie and humor and less stress, employee absence, and turnover.

How to Recognize Good Cooperation

When cooperation in a work group is high, there is a discernible positive attitude. Members responsibly handle their own assignments and willingly volunteer to help each other—even before they are asked. Problems are addressed with much energy and creativity. There is spontaneous brainstorming and a free exchange of ideas. While members may speak passionately for their positions, all important decisions are made by consensus, not by voting. Once consensus is reached, every member supports the action. Conflicts are managed through win/win negotiations; once they are addressed, they are let go—there is little rehashing of old disputes. Compliments, recognition, and celebrations are commonplace; members speak with pride about "their team."

Although each work team might list slightly different indicators of cooperation, five elements seem to be common across work groups. To assess the level of cooperation within your team, consider the cooperation F.A.C.T.S.—Follow-through, Accuracy, Creativity, Timeliness, and Spirit. They are good indicators that cooperation is high.

Follow-Through

One of the most common phrases heard in a group that works well together is, "You can count on it." Members trust that when a commitment is made to return a phone call, read a report, talk to a customer, attend a meeting, or change a behavior, the job will be done. There will be follow-through. When work associates are cooperating, they follow through on promises and demonstrate a keen awareness that as part of a team, everything they do impacts someone else. It is clear to these team members that if they forget to do something, they become a weak link, an obstacle in the work process. Lack of follow-through blocks the performance of others and reduces trust. It is impossible to trust people who do not do what they say they will do. Lack of follow-through may also be interpreted as a lack of consideration for others since it is boring to "remind" adult colleagues that something is due, and annoying to sit through meetings where excuses are offered about why things were not done. When individuals don't do what they say, it is demoralizing and leads to a rather contagious lack of effort. On the other hand, when team members keep commitments, they inspire their colleagues to do the same.

Accuracy

Another common phrase heard in cooperative work groups is, "We do it right the first time." Accuracy is not just a reflection of personal pride but a reflection of a commitment to uphold standards of a work group, to contribute to group pride. It indicates that team members take their work seriously and are giving their best effort. Accuracy also indicates a respect for the time of others, which is a critical element of cooperation. When cooperation is high, individuals take the time to think before acting and to inspect work before presenting it. By doing so members demonstrate that they care about the team and that work for the team is a priority. In work groups where cooperation is high, members expend a special effort for the good of the team and inspire others to do the same.

Creativity

Another indicator of team cooperation is widespread creativity. Innovative thinking flourishes when individuals feel secure and supported by their colleagues. Although taking the lead in a new order of things is risky business, such risk is greatly reduced in a cooperative environment where members forgive mistakes, forget transgressions, and respect individual differences.

When cooperation is high, members don't look for excuses about why things can't be done. Instead they use their creativity to solve productivity problems, meet customer needs, and find new ways of helping each other. Everyone looks for ways to make things happen. Individuals ask, "How can I help make that happen?" instead of itemizing all the reasons why they can't. Problems are approached as opportunities and are often resolved with spontaneous group brainstorming. Ideas flow freely and there are no naysayers. Individuals build on each other's thoughts without the guardedness that accompanies a low-cooperation environment. Lists of ideas are generated before evaluation of any particular ideas begin. Good-natured humor is prevalent. The relaxed, non-threatening atmosphere that accompanies high cooperation allows people to have fun and to risk doing things differently. The results are often much better than any one team member could produce on his or her own. The synergy created by building on each other's ideas moves the group to a new level of innovation.

Timeliness

Attention to timeliness is also an indicator of high cooperation. When members are truly cooperating, they are respectful of each other's time. People are on time for appointments; meetings begin and end on time. Phone calls are returned promptly. Task assignments are completed as promised. There is a sense of urgency about team tasks, reflecting a willingness to make team commitments top priorities.

Important information is shared promptly and succinctly. Members are asked for input regularly but not so often that it blocks efficiency. Individuals tend to "cluster" their questions and comments so that they share them all at once instead of repeatedly interrupting each other's work day. Individual schedules are known, and personal planning time is respected. Important group activities are scheduled so that everyone can attend. You might also note people thanking each other for their time or asking, "Is this a good time?" It is hard not to cooperate with those who respect your time.

Spirit

Being on a work team is a bit like being part of a family. You can't have your way all of the time. To make it work, all parties must have a generous spirit. When cooperation is high in a group, a positive attitude prevails. Members value individual differences, speak kindly about individual talents, offer compliments on individual contributions—but also form a team identity. Members develop mutual trust, communicate openly, and willingly welcome new members as needed.

Differences are managed through win/win negotiating. Members show flexibility, an ability to compromise, and a willingness to work for mutual good. In a highly cooperative group, there are few turf wars, little competitiveness, and an ability to forgive and forget.

FOCUS ON TIMELINESS
- create urgency about team tasks
- give team commitments priority

Improvement **TIP**

RULES OF TEAM SPIRIT
- value the individual
- develop team trust
- communicate openly
- manage differences
- share successes
- welcome new members

When there is good team spirit, decisions are made by consensus, not by voting. Voting divides a team into winners and losers; consensus forges interdependence. Reaching consensus requires each member to cooperate by listening to each point of view, modifying his or her own position to accommodate the will of the group, and supporting the decision which seems best for the group.

When spirited cooperation is high, celebrations are frequent and often spontaneous. Members may recognize special occasions such as birthdays or weddings, individual accomplishments such as successful presentations or promotions, or team successes such as new performance records or achievement awards. Recognition on such occasions may be as informal as someone bringing in donuts or pizza, or as formal as presenting framed certificates. The congratulations are always sincere, however, and the message is explicitly clear: "We celebrate each other's milestones and successes because we are all on the same team. A win for one is a win for all." Such camaraderie is a good sign that cooperation within the group is high.

What Can You Do To Enhance Cooperation?

2 INDIVIDUAL IMPROVEMENT STRATEGIES

1. **Be a positive role model.**
2. **Ask colleagues for feedback.**

Be a Positive Role Model

Don't do unto others as they do unto you. Do unto others as you *wish* they would do unto you. You may have heard the expression, "What goes around, comes around." This is especially true in work groups. Cooperation—or a lack of cooperation—can be very contagious.

If you want more cooperation from others, try giving more cooperation yourself. If others are not returning phone calls promptly, set an example by being very prompt in returning your calls. If others are rigid in their demands, try being especially flexible about your requests. Just trust that when you "do the right thing," you encourage others to follow your example. And even if a few do not follow, you will be in a much better position to negotiate if you have been cooperating yourself.

To determine how you can become an even more positive role model grade yourself on the F.A.C.T.S. of cooperation. If your total score is less than an "A", try using cooperation behaviors you have not tried and/or increasing the frequency of cooperation behaviors you presently use.

F.A.C.T.S. of Cooperation

Grade yourself on each cooperation subject below by entering the number that best identifies how often you behave as described: 4=usually, 3=often, 2=sometimes, and 1=seldom.

[ ] 1. Follow-through
   (*Return phone calls, keep commitments, do what I say I am going to do*)

[ ] 2. Accuracy
   (*Pay attention to detail, check facts, proof my writing, rehearse presentations, seldom have "redos"*)

[ ] 3. Creativity
   (*Approach problems positively, listen openly to new ideas, suggest different ways of doing things, offer specific ways I can contribute to the team*)

[ ] 4. Timeliness
   (*Meet deadlines, arrive on time, speak succinctly, cluster questions for others, show respect for other's time*)

[ ] 5. Spirit
   (*Pitch in to help, show appreciation for others, think win/win to manage differences, remain flexible in consensus decision making, celebrate with others, add humor or fun*)

Total cooperation score:_____

A=21–25   B=16–20   C=11–15   D=Below 11

Ask Colleagues For Feedback

Since honest feedback is seldom volunteered and since, like most human beings, you probably are not very objective about your own behavior, you may be uncooperative and not even be aware of it. Feedback on the results of your behavior provides you with a reality check. It can also help you regulate your behavior. Feedback should be from a credible, trusted source. A credible source is someone who has first-hand knowledge of your

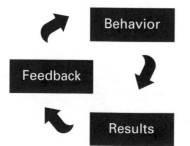

behavior. A trusted source is someone you believe has your best interests at heart and will not be unreasonably critical of you (like someone you just edged out of a promotion).

Since most of your team members find it difficult to provide honest feedback, you can make it easier by stating why you want it and by phrasing the request positively. First, let colleagues know that you are really interested in contributing to a higher cooperation level on the team and that their opinions are important to you. Second, instead of saying, "Tell me what I do wrong," ask, "How can I be even more cooperative?" Also remember that giving feedback is a big risk, so reinforce the person, even if you don't like what you hear. A good rule when receiving feedback is to count to five before saying anything at all. Then just say, "Thank you for your insight. I'll really think about what you said." This strategy will help you avoid becoming defensive, even in the face of negative feedback.

THREE WAYS TO GET FEEDBACK

- explain why you want it
- phrase the request positively
- count to five

You might also ask a few trusted team members to discuss your F.A.C.T.S. report card. This will help you to see if your perceptions of how you cooperate match what others think about you.

Improvement **TIP**

By asking for feedback on your own behavior, you can enhance the cooperation level of your group in two ways. First, you will learn what you can do personally to increase cooperation, and second, you will encourage others to think about their own cooperative behaviors.

What Can Your Team Do To Enhance Cooperation?

5 TEAM IMPROVEMENT STRATEGIES

1. **Assess present cooperation level.**

2. **Target a few improvement areas.**

3. **Develop consensus-building techniques.**

4. **Reinforce team cooperation.**

5. **Encourage interpersonal activities.**

Assess Present Cooperation Level

To get an honest reading on the level of cooperation in your group, you might invite a consultant (internal or external) to interview team members privately. This would be particularly helpful if trust is low or tension is high. Otherwise, to determine what members think of your group's cooperation level, you can conduct an informal survey. Just bring everyone together, distribute a survey, and ask that everyone complete it privately. Collect the unsigned surveys, tally the answers on a master sheet, and post the results on newsprint. Ask individuals to jot down any observations about the data (surprises, connections, possible reasons for the results) before any group discussion. Then discuss what behaviors your team should continue, which you should eliminate, and which you should add. Develop a survey using questions similar to those in TEAM ACTIVITY 11: TEAM COOPERATION SURVEY*, adding any other questions your group feels are important.

*Reproducible masters of Team Activity 11 and all other individual and team activities in this book can be found in *50 Activities For Teams At Work*, Suzanne Willis Zoglio, Tower Hill Press, Doylestown, PA.

TEAM COOPERATION SURVEY

For each item below, rate your work team on a scale of 4 to 1:
4=strongly agree, 3=agree, 2=disagree, 1=strongly disagree.

[ ]   1.   We are on time for meetings.

[ ]   2.   We consider individual schedules when planning group
           events.

[ ]   3.   Members return phone calls promptly.

[ ]   4.   Assignments are completed as promised.

[ ]   5.   We show creativity in our problem solving.

[ ]   6.   Members regularly offer to help each other.

[ ]   7.   Conflict is not avoided, but managed with a win/win mindset.

[ ]   8.   All important decisions are made by consensus.

[ ]   9.   We often celebrate together.

[ ] 10.   Cooperation is high in this work group.

[ ] 11.   _____

[ ] 12.   _____

[ ] 13.   _____

[ ] 14.   _____

[ ] 15.   _____

Target a Few Improvement Areas

To ensure the highest probability of success in enhancing team cooperation, focus on only one or two behaviors that need improvement. You might do this by first listing (and numbering) on newsprint any items from your team cooperation survey which were rated low by at least 25% of your work group. This is your "short list" of cooperation behaviors to improve. Now ask each member to vote for the two behaviors he or she would most like to see improved. Tally the written votes, post the answers, and circle the two items with the highest votes. These are team

Improvement
TIP

priorities—areas to be developed first. Spend some time discussing how to improve these priority cooperation areas. For a seven-step guide to targeting improvement areas see TEAM ACTIVITY 12: COOPERATION TACTICS.

---

team activity

12   COOPERATION TACTICS

Complete the questions below.

1. List any team cooperation survey items from TEAM ACTIVITY 11 rated 1 or 2 by 25% of your group.

2. List the two items from above which received the most votes for needing attention immediately:
    A:
    B:

3. Discuss ways to improve item A.

4. Discuss ways to improve item B.

5. List actions (ground rules) you all agree to follow in order to improve the above two items.

6. Set a date to check progress.

7. Decide who will ensure that you monitor progress.

Develop Consensus-Building Techniques

Your team can learn techniques for building group consensus by bringing in an outside trainer, using an internal trainer, or sending a representative to a seminar. Check with human resources, staff development, or training for suggestions. As mentioned earlier, voting divides a team into two camps—winners and losers. Consensus encourages groups to work issues through to basic agreement.

Consensus does not mean unanimous agreement but it does mean that each person can honestly say, "I have been listened to fairly, and I can live with this decision. While it may not be my first choice, I will support the group's decision." Obviously, consensus requires individual team members to put aside their personal interests and consider what is best for the team. Members must be flexible and reasonable, resisting the temptation to satisfy their individual egos at a cost to the team.

There are many techniques for developing consensus in a group (e.g., brainstorming, multi-voting, nominal group technique). *The Team Handbook* by Peter Scholtes, et al., provides good resource material on these techniques as does the Pfeiffer and Jones series, *Structured Experiences*, available from Pfeiffer & Company, San Diego, California. When teams learn techniques for consensus decision making, cooperation is greatly enhanced.

Reinforce Team Cooperation

Teams can recognize cooperative individuals in a number of ways. At team meetings you can add a "kudos" section to your agenda in order to verbally mention cooperative behaviors. In team newsletters you can spotlight special efforts. The team can award big C (for cooperation) mugs, tee shirts, or cafeteria dollars.

You can enhance one-on-one recognition of cooperative behavior by agreeing as a group that each team member will recognize at least one colleague a week with a personal appreciation award. Some groups use stars, small plaques,

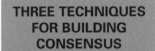

CONSENSUS MEANS

- **everyone is heard**
- **all can support a decision**

THREE TECHNIQUES FOR BUILDING CONSENSUS

- **brainstorming**
- **multi-voting**
- **nominal groups**

Improvement
TIP

roses, sweet treats, lunch gift certificates, personal citations, limericks, songs, and life-size greeting cards. With a little imagination your group can create your own awards, perhaps even changing them monthly. The award itself is not as important as the ceremony. It should sincerely recognize outstanding examples of cooperation within the team.

Improvement
TIP

To determine what behaviors should be recognized, agree as a group what behaviors enhance trust. Then agree to focus on especially recognizing those behaviors.

Encourage Interpersonal Activities

Most of us know very little about our work associates except what they do at work. Yet, relationships are built on trust, and trust is enhanced when we know and respect each other as multifaceted individuals. When others know the personal challenges we face (e.g., health battles, losses, single-parenting challenges, graduate-school pressures), they have a better understanding of the whole person. Therefore, it is important to orchestrate opportunities for team members to get to know about each other's life outside of work. TEAM ACTIVITY 13: TEAM-BUILDING IDEAS provides some suggestions for building a more cohesive team. Use this list as a springboard for generating ideas of your own.

team activity

13   TEAM-BUILDING IDEAS

Consider the following ideas for your group.

✶ Have a team family day (or lunch) at work.

✶ Schedule a retreat once or twice a year where you go off-site for a team-building meeting.

✶ Establish a written profile each month where one member interviews another and then writes up a V.I.P. profile to be posted, distributed, or included in a department newsletter. The profile would focus on little known facts, talents, thoughts, hobbies, dreams, etc.

✶ Have a "mystery baby" day where a bulletin board displays baby photos and others have to guess the team members represented, where they were born, and how many siblings they have.

✶ Have an "On The Light Side" bulletin board where team members can contribute jokes, stories, cartoons, or motivational comments.

✶ Sponsor a "retirement fantasy" contest where members submit their future dreams without names. Other members play detective to match members with their dreams.

✶ Produce a team talent show for a local retirement community.

✶ Adopt a needy family and refurbish their home as a team project...one room a year.

✶ Start a team prose and poetry collection.

✶ Have a quarterly team sports day (wallyball, softball, roller skating).

✶ Hold game tournaments (Songburst, Pictionary, Charades, Chess, Trivial Pursuit, etc.) over lunch every now and then. Playoffs can be between departments, shifts, etc.

✶ Hold a department arts and crafts show.

✶ Plan a department field trip (e.g., day at the museum, amusement park, hiking, biking, tubing).

✶ Hold a department cook-off (best chili, chocolate chip cookies, brownies, etc.)

Yours: _____

Some of the team-building ideas you generate may be one-time events (e.g., mystery baby day, retirement fantasy contest), while others may become traditions (e.g., semi-annual retreat, team holiday talent show, spring game tournament). The important thing is to create regular opportunities where team members can learn more about each other, develop appreciation for each member's uniqueness, and understand what members share in common.

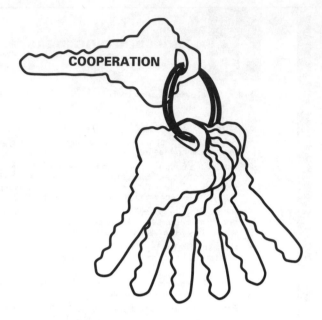

COOPERATION

CHAPTER 4
SUMMARY

- Teams need cooperation in order to remain flexible, responsive, and efficient.

- When cooperation is high, team members follow through on commitments, produce high quality work, creatively solve problems, respect each other's time, and exhibit strong team spirit.

- Team members can enhance cooperation by being positive role models and by seeking feedback from colleagues on how to cooperate even more.

- Teams can enhance cooperation by assessing and improving present levels of team cooperation, reinforcing cooperative actions, developing consensus-building techniques, and encouraging interpersonal activities.

"Diplomacy: The art of jumping into troubled waters without making a splash."

Art Linkletter

CONFLICT MANAGEMENT

NOTES

It is inevitable that any team of strong-willed individuals will experience interpersonal conflict from time to time. In fact, the surfacing of some conflict is actually a positive sign, since it indicates diversity of thinking. What is not positive, however, is ongoing conflict that is tolerated, not managed. A festering conflict not only drains energy from conflicting parties but also wastes time, creates tension in the work group, and presents real obstacles to innovative problem solving.

If you have ever worked in a situation where colleagues did not get along, you know all too well how debilitating unmanaged conflict can be. Warring parties create undue tension in the work group by attempting to get others on their side and against the other party. They bad-mouth colleagues, make snide remarks in meetings, and continue an underground campaign. They do not confront the conflict responsibly. Such individuals generally lack interpersonal skills, negotiation skills, or the motivation to change. Ongoing unmanaged conflict reflects

"You can't hold a man down without staying down with him."

Booker T. Washington

poorly on both parties, often affecting future career opportunities. Since no conflict can continue without fanning from both directions, such conflicts also rob both parties—in fact the entire team—of energy. Energy is lost and time is wasted when individuals talk about each other, make each other look bad, take ridiculous measures to avoid each other, or try to seduce fellow workers into "back-me" campaigns.

Perhaps you have tried to help colleagues resolve a conflict. You may have considered locking the warring individuals in a room and making them "duke" it out, once and for all. Or maybe you planned on mediating a settlement yourself, then shied away in fear that both parties would stop speaking to you. You could easily have used that time to plan your week, take a professional development course, or interact with constituents—all of the things you never have enough time for. Conflict between two parties is definitely everybody's business, and conflict management is critical to team success.

Unmanaged conflict blocks the development of team trust because it is often accompanied by backstabbing, gossip, pettiness, and a lack of responsibility for keeping the conflict going. Low trust blocks the playful, spontaneous atmosphere necessary for creative thought and innovative problem solving.

On the contrary, groups that manage conflict well report more innovative problem solving as well as higher productivity, less stress, and greater job satisfaction. These groups expect differences. In fact, they even encourage open expression of differences. But they *manage* those differences quickly and fairly, under the ground rules of win/win negotiating.

RESULTS OF UNMANAGED CONFLICT

- gossip
- backstabbing
- pettiness
- low trust
- tension

How to Recognize Good Conflict Management

In work groups where conflict is managed well, you will observe little gossip and backbiting. There is no need to talk behind an individual's back because differences are addressed responsibly face to face. You will also notice less tension and more playfulness. When individuals are in harmony with each other, they have more confidence and take more risks, such as sharing personal stories, looking silly, and generally having fun.

You may also notice what seems to be unusually direct communication, both positive and negative. Individuals risk saying what they think when they think it. They have learned that early confrontation means a quicker resolution because less emotional baggage is involved. Although their talk is direct, it will not reflect the hostility which typically builds when hurt feelings are allowed to accumulate and then blurted out all at once. Any criticism will seem less personal, more issue-oriented. As individuals learn to manage conflict, the process becomes less personal, less emotional.

Also, when conflict is managed well, participation at meetings is high and there are few hidden agendas or individuals trying to monopolize the spotlight. Suggestions are numerous and brainstorming occurs quite spontaneously. People seem to build on each other's ideas, focusing on what parts they *like* instead of nitpicking the pieces they don't like. Everyone seems to be working toward a win/win solution—one that is satisfactory to all and where there are no losers. Team members focus on the discussion at hand rather than on personal differences. When you find a team that manages conflict well, you will be able to say, "They know how to disagree agreeably. They may reject ideas, but they respect individuals."

What Can You Do
To Enhance Conflict Management?

4 INDIVIDUAL IMPROVEMENT STRATEGIES

1. **Understand your own conflict style.**

2. **Improve your conflict management skills.**

3. **Take the first step.**

4. **Encourage colleagues to resolve differences.**

Understand Your Own Conflict Style

Just as some people are assertive communicators and others are nonassertive, some people are more assertive conflict managers and others are more collaborative. Since all styles of conflict management are appropriate at certain times, there really is no right or wrong style. However, some styles are more effective with certain people and in certain situations. The only way you can consciously choose the most appropriate style is to be aware of your own "default" style... the style you use automatically. In order to find out your style, you might complete a conflict management style inventory such as the *Thomas-Kilmann Conflict Mode Instrument* developed by Kenneth W. Thomas and Ralph H. Kilmann, available from Xicom Inc., Tuxedo, New York. This self-scoring instrument contains a description of five different styles, the strengths and weaknesses of each, and the situations for which each style is useful.

Improve Your Conflict Management Skills

To better manage conflict you should be able to shift your paradigm (a mindset or mental model) about conflict situations in general, about the other party, and about your own competencies. A paradigm reveals certain assumptions about what you consider to be true. For instance, if you believe that most people are basically selfish and only interested in getting what they want, you are operating under a particular paradigm. Since paradigms can be subjective, outdated, or incorrect, they may stifle creative negotiating and should be examined carefully. Shifting your paradigm will increase your chances of resolving a conflict because it allows you to see things differently. Consider these historical figures who have helped us see our world differently:

- Columbus...who showed us that the world is round, not flat.
- Pasteur...who proved that invisible things (bacteria) can kill you.
- Yeager...who broke the sound barrier and did not disintegrate.

It is important to check your paradigms.

Check Your Paradigm

Belief systems can be real obstacles because they limit our view of what's possible, probable, or necessary. Therefore, before trying to resolve any conflict, check your mindset. By doing so, you will identify any biased thinking that might block a successful resolution.

1. What mindset might you have about conflict situations in general?

    Example: "Before a conflict is over, one person has to win and one lose."

    Yours: _____

    _____

2. Think about a conflict you presently need to resolve. What mindset might you have about the "other" party?

    Example: "The only way to get through to him is to firmly state what I want and not give him an inch. Otherwise, he'll walk all over me."

    Yours: _____

    _____

3. What mindset do you have about yourself in that situation?

    Example: "There is nothing I can do about this situation; my hands are tied. We'll probably end up in a shouting match, because that woman really makes me see red."

    Yours: _____

    _____

THREE TECHNIQUES TO CHANGE PARADIGMS

- **reframing**
- **shifting shoes**
- **affirmations**

Three techniques that will help you shift from a negative paradigm to a more positive one are reframing, shifting shoes, and using affirmations. Improving these skills provides you with an opportunity to mentally move from a closed perspective to a more open perspective that enhances the probability of succeeding with win/win conflict management.

When you are skilled in reframing, you can actually see a situation from a different vantage point. As a child, you might have used a kaleidoscope. You would turn it to rearrange the parts and form a different picture. You adjusted it to create a different view. To become a more effective negotiator, it is sometimes helpful to "reframe" things, that is, to see them a little differently. Reframing is a bit like describing the glass as "half full" instead of "half empty." It is seeing the bright side or taking a more positive point of view.

Reframing Your Thoughts

Reframing is a technique you can use to change your mindset about a conflict situation.

Example:

Before Reframing	**After Reframing**
It's either him or me.	*We can both win.*
The situation is hopeless.	*A solution is possible.*
We shouldn't have conflict.	*Conflict is to be expected.*

Try reframing these thoughts:

A. It's not worth the hassle to confront her with what she said.

Reframe:

B. If I make any concessions, I'll look weak and he'll walk all over me.

Reframe:

C. Hey, I didn't start this thing—she did. So why should I negotiate?

Reframe:

Improvement
TIP

A second technique for shifting your mindset, particularly about another person, is to try mentally walking in the other person's shoes. When you do so, you are practicing empathy, seeing things from the other person's point of view.

Shifting Shoes

Walking in someone else's shoes requires empathy. You must feel what the other person feels, see things the other person sees. It is not an easy skill to learn, but practice definitely helps.

1. What might one of your team members be feeling when he gets chewed out in front of others?

2. How might your boss view a lack of volunteers for the quality task force?

3. How might the person with whom you are in conflict be feeling?

4. What is really important to that person; what are his/her interests?

A third technique that helps with paradigm shifting (particularly about yourself) is using affirmations (positive self-talk). An affirmation is a positive statement made in the present tense about something you want to be true. You play affirmations over and over in your head, like a tape, to replace any negative thoughts.

For example, suppose you are nervous about bringing up a conflict with someone. Running through your mind are negative thoughts like, "I know I'll blow up," or, "I won't be able to stand up for my rights," or, "I'm so nervous I'll probably forget everything." You can replace these negative thoughts with affirmations such as:

- "I am calm, prepared, and capable of negotiating."
- "I am controlled, assertive, and flexible."

AFFIRMATIONS ARE

- **positive**
- **in the present tense**

Using Affirmations

Think about a conflict you are presently experiencing. What negative thoughts about the conflict might you be playing over and over in your mind?

Write one affirmation that you could mentally repeat instead:

To get the most out of your affirmations, repeat them several times during the day, particularly when you get up in the morning and just before you go to sleep. Some individuals find that writ-

ing an affirmation on a Post-It™ Note allows them to keep the affirmation visible all day. You could post one on your mirror, appointment book, dashboard, or key case.

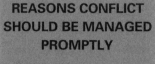

REASONS CONFLICT
SHOULD BE MANAGED
PROMPTLY

• facts fade

• emotions build

Take the First Step

The most difficult step in conflict resolution is often the first step. Verbally acknowledging to another person that the two of you have a problem is not easy. The tendency is to put it off. But as you put it off, it becomes more difficult to resolve the situation because facts fade, incidents get mentally rewritten, and wounds fester. When you deal with conflict promptly—hopefully within 48 hours of the conflict—you make it easier on yourself. To prepare for discussion, write down what is bothering you, specific examples of where it occurs, and why it bothers you.

To become more of a resolution initiator, promise yourself that whenever you experience conflict with a colleague, you will take the first step by going to that person to arrange a meeting where you can discuss the problem. By doing so, you will contribute to positive group norms and help others break the avoidance habit. You will positively impact your group's ability to resolve differences and maintain an open work climate.

Encourage Colleagues to Resolve Differences

Conducting business as usual while individuals have unresolved conflict inadvertently reinforces conflict avoidance. Since behaviors which are accepted are generally repeated, and behaviors which are ignored are generally considered acceptable, any conflict that is ignored is likely to continue. To avoid such long-term conflict, talk about the conflict to the parties involved. If you notice tension between two team members, approach one of the members and explain how the tensions are affecting you personally and the team as a whole. Since individuals often rationalize putting off conflict negotiation by thinking they are not hurting anyone but themselves, your comments may help shed some light on the fact that interpersonal conflicts block team communication, cooperation, and creativity.

You might even suggest to your colleague a method for initiating the negotiation. Perhaps you could offer an outline of steps or share a success story of your own, relaying what you did and said that worked in your situation. If your colleague is really nervous, you could even offer to mediate the first conference, or suggest an objective facilitator (perhaps a training or human resource specialist).

If you don't see any change in the relationship, ask again if the individual has initiated a negotiation. Don't give up, and don't allow the individual to convince you that it is none of your business and that you should "butt out." Talk about your team's commitment to be open and honest and your group's desire to work within a positive, pleasant environment. Be firm in your belief that differences within the group must be worked out as they occur if your work team is to reach its full potential.

Unmanaged conflict affects team communication, cooperation, and creativity.

Improvement
TIP

What Can Your Team Do
To Enhance Conflict Management?

3 TEAM
IMPROVEMENT
STRATEGIES

1. **Establish related ground rules.**

2. **Take conflict management training.**

3. **Agree on a model to use.**

Establish Related Ground Rules

Your team should agree on ground rules for responding to team conflict. Such rules might include time guidelines (e.g., "when conflict occurs, the parties will set a date to negotiate differences within a week"), or courtesy rules (e.g., "differences will be handled privately, not in team meetings"), or strategies to use when ongoing conflict is observed (e.g., "when a conflict continues unmanaged, observers will provide responsible feedback to the involved parties").

You can develop conflict management ground rules in just a meeting or two. If your organization has trained group facilitators, ask one to conduct the meeting. If not, consider hiring an external consultant, "borrow" someone from another organization, or ask a neutral party from another department to act as facilitator, following a process similar to the one outlined in TEAM ACTIVITY 14: ESTABLISHING GROUND RULES.*

---

*Reproducible masters of Team Activity 14 and all other individual and team activities in this book can be found in *50 Activities For Teams At Work*, Suzanne Willis Zoglio, Tower Hill Press, Doylestown, PA.

14 ESTABLISHING GROUND RULES

Follow the seven steps presented below to establish ground rules for effectively managing conflict.

Step 1: Solicit individual thoughts.

To be sure that individual ideas are represented, ask each team member to list on large 8" x 12" cards (file folders cut in half will do) two or three possible conflict management rules—one rule per card. Ask each person to be succinct and to use abbreviations for this first round.

Step 2: Cluster rules by similar themes.

After five to ten minutes, collect the cards and display them on a wall in the room. Use Post-it™ glue stick or masking tape so that you can move the cards around. As the group reviews the cards, cluster those that are similar so that you end up with rules for five or six categories (e.g., time, privacy, process, observer, group reinforcement).

Step 3: Form small groups to refine rules in each category.

Form small groups by counting off or by identifying interest in a category, and assign a category to each group. Ask each sub-group to read all of the rules offered for their category, and try to refine them into one or two representative rules. Allow 20 minutes, then ask each group to write their representative rules on large flip chart paper that can be taped up for the whole group to see.

Team Activity 14 continues...

Take Conflict Management Training

The best way to enhance conflict management skills within the team is to take a seminar together where you can learn a model and modify it for your group. There are many such courses offered by independent consultants, local colleges and universities, or possibly your own training department. Check with your Human Resources Department for any company-sponsored programs. Explore options, ask to review materials, and check client references. If limited resources prohibit a seminar for the group, you might agree on a book that you will all read and discuss. There are also video tape

Team Activity 14 continued.

Step 4: Gain consensus on ground rules.

In the large group, hold a discussion of the new ground rules, asking for suggestions in wording but reminding people that you are seeking *general* agreement, not clarification or semantics at this point. The question each member should answer is, "Can I support this ground rule? If not, how can I modify it so I could support it?"

Step 5: Discuss obstacles to using ground rules.

Form new subgroups by asking two or three people from each group to move clockwise to the next group. Ask each new group to list anything that might make it hard for some people to live up to the ground rules that were just agreed upon (e.g., out-of-town travel will make it hard to set up meetings within 48 hours of conflict). After 20 minutes, ask each group to report one concern at a time, listening to all groups before going back to the first one. Record each potential obstacle on newsprint until all concerns are represented.

Step 6: Brainstorm how to minimize obstacles.

Discuss how to limit obstacles. You might even need to modify a rule (e.g., change a time limit from 48 hours to one work week), or to develop implementation strategies (e.g., use voice mail, call at home, meet before or after work).

Step 7: Poll the group for commitment to ground rules.

Ask each person to state his or her commitment to the newly created ground rules.

Improvement **TIP**

programs and audio tape programs. Your library, the American Society for Training and Development, and your Chamber of Commerce are possible referral sources for training professionals and suppliers of packaged training programs.

Agree on a Model to Use

There are several models of conflict management that support win/win solutions. Each outlines specific steps to follow when you want to work out a mutually satisfying solution to an interpersonal conflict.

Which conflict management model you decide to use is not as important as agreeing to follow the same basic model whenever there is an interpersonal conflict on your team. Once basic steps are agreed upon, there will be less fear related to opening up a discussion, and there will be more personal confidence in the ability to control the interaction. Even motivated individuals avoid addressing conflict if they fear losing control or lack knowledge on how to reach a mutually acceptable solution. When a group agrees to use a particular model, individuals can anticipate how an interaction will proceed. Fear of the unknown is diminished because the process has already been agreed upon. It is only a matter of proceeding through each step. Both parties know the destination (a mutually acceptable solution) and the process (steps in the model). When a team agrees to use a conflict management model, group conflict diminishes.

You can learn such models by taking a course, listening to negotiating tapes, reading books such as, *Getting To Yes* by Fisher and Ury or *Getting Past No* by William Ury. One model is outlined for you in TEAM ACTIVITY 15: SIX STEPS TO MANAGING CONFLICT (see page 82). Perhaps you will find it useful in and of itself, or as a foundation for a model of your own.

Remember, however, that no model will be successful unless both individuals are motivated to work out a win/win solution. In other words, there must be a *benefit* if they manage the conflict and/or some discomfort if they don't. Team leader influence and peer pressure can go a long way in creating the motivation to manage conflict. The steps in managing conflict are not as important as an honorable intent and a collaborative attitude. The goal is to find a *mutually satisfying solution* through a process that leaves long-term relationships intact. If you push your way through the process, demanding that only your needs be met, you may win the battle but you will definitely lose the war. Win/win negotiation requires an ability to identify what you want, a willingness to listen to what the other party wants, and a commitment to work out a mutually satisfying solution.

Improvement **TIP**

team activity

15 SIX STEPS TO MANAGING CONFLICT

Step 1: Shift your paradigm (your mindset).
- Reframe the situation (look at the bright side)
- Practice empathy/objectivity about the other party
- Use affirmations (positive mental messages) about your own competencies

Step 2: Emphasize what you have in common.
- "We both want..."
- "Neither of us wants..."
- "We have a problem to work out..."

Step 3: State your win/win intent.
- "I'd like to find a solution that will work for both of us."
- "Are you willing to work with me on finding a solution we can both feel good about?"
- "Perhaps we can agree on how we can work toward agreement?"

Step 4: Generate alternatives together.
- "What if we...?"
- "Suppose we were to try...?"

Step 5: Decide on the best solution(s).
- "Any ideas acceptable to both of us?"
- "Any ideas we could modify to make acceptable?"
- "Then it looks like we should try..."

Step 6: Plan the implementation.
- Decide on the best solution
- Plan a time to check progress

CHAPTER 5

SUMMARY

- Teams need to accept conflict as normal and manage it well in order to be productive and maintain job satisfaction.

- When conflict is well managed, teams demonstrate an open trust that allows risk taking and supports objective decision making and problem solving.

- Members can enhance conflict management by understanding their own style, improving skills, initiating conflict resolution, and encouraging colleagues to manage their differences.

- Teams can enhance conflict management by establishing ground rules for managing differences, taking conflict management training, and agreeing on a specific model the team will use.

CHAPTER

6

"The surviving companies will, above all, be flexible responders that create market initiatives. This has to happen through people."

Tom Peters
Thriving on Chaos

CHANGE MANAGEMENT

NOTES

In the fast-paced, competitive world of the nineties, organizations must become highly responsive if they expect to survive. Customer priorities change, government regulations change, technology changes, competition changes, and taxpayer demands change. Only organizations which remain flexible, foster innovation, and develop skill in managing transitions will succeed. It is no longer a luxury to have work teams which can perform effectively within a turbulent environment. It is a necessity.

Work teams must remain flexible to develop improved processes for enhancing quality, containing costs, and creating a positive work climate. Teams increasingly are asked to generate creative solutions, develop improved services or products, and identify more efficient procedures. The new norm in excellent organizations is to focus on continuous improvement—abandoning the concept that "there is one best way," and embracing the concept that "there is always a way to be better." To be effective, work teams must adopt a new paradigm about expectations at work. They need to shift their thinking from "change is unusual; it is something unexpected" to "change is quite normal; it is a necessary constant." Along with embracing such a mind-set, teams need to develop skills associated with the management of change.

Change in the workplace is here to stay. If work teams do not manage change well, they may find themselves without jobs, without input, or without support from their constituency. They may also lose good team players due to the stress of poorly managed change, which lowers morale and increases turnover. Either way, the team loses. On the other hand, teams that manage change well help their organizations stay competitive, attract and retain good personnel, and enjoy a higher quality work life.

How to Recognize Good Change Management

When teams develop effective change management skills, members exhibit several behaviors. They set goals, measure performance, and plan for improvement. Individuals are curious about how well the team and the organization are doing against stated goals, and they seem energetic about accomplishing even more. There is no defensive justification for mediocre results. Instead there is plenty of brainstorming about how to improve the process. In groups which manage change well there is little need to deny performance feedback (and its implication for change) because there is little fear of change. When individuals know how to manage something, it no longer poses a threat. Fear of the unknown diminishes with each change that is well managed.

When change management is high, energy is often high due to new challenges and regular stimulation. When change management skills are poor, opportunities are often avoided, the status quo is encouraged, and energy lags.

Change is often like a double-edged sword, bringing with it both fear and excitement. In fact, the Chinese symbol for change (crisis) is composed of two characters; one represents danger, the other represents opportunity.

With good change management skills, teams perceive change as a challenging opportunity instead of a danger to avoid. Team members demonstrate a high level of directed energy. "Directed energy," however, is not the same as "crazy-as-a-loon" energy where individuals seem nearly certifiable. Directed energy is focused energy that could be described as *vitality* or *excitement*.

Excitement turns to creativity in a work group where change is managed well. When individuals are skilled in dealing with change, they are more open to ideas and more apt to consider them on merit rather than on how much discomfort they might cause. Innovation, creative problem solving, and creative humor are all associated with a work team that is comfortable riding the waves of change.

If a team is prosperous in a turbulent work environment, be assured that change management is high. Such teams set the pace for the rest of an organization. Team members dream, plan, and act. Risk taking is commonplace and mistakes are considered worthwhile lessons.

The Chinese symbol for crisis represents danger and opportunity.

What Can You Do
To Enhance Change Management?

3 INDIVIDUAL IMPROVEMENT STRATEGIES

1. **Identify the benefits.**

2. **Experiment with open thinking.**

3. **Talk positively about change.**

PERSONAL BENEFITS OF MANAGING CHANGE

- **job security**
- **career advancement**
- **improved marketability**
- **increased job satisfaction**

Identify the Benefits

One of the best ways to influence effective change management within your group is to become more open to change yourself. Since no one changes a behavior without an incentive, you might identify the benefits you will experience if you become a better change manager. Then when you find yourself tempted to cling to old behaviors, you will be able to focus on the potential gain of the change instead of on any associated discomfort. It is a bit like starting a new exercise program or giving up smoking. Each requires that you give up something comfortable in order to gain something you want. To stick with any new regimen, you must believe that the gain is worth the pain.

So if you work to become a better change manager yourself, and if you work at helping your whole team develop such skills, what are the benefits to you? Four obvious benefits are: job security, career advancement, improved marketability, and increased job satisfaction.

Job security is a benefit of good change management in two ways. First, as mentioned earlier, organizations that are flexible and responsive will flourish. When organizations flourish, jobs, in general, are more secure. Second, as you become more adept at change, you become personally more valuable, especially if your organization is committed to continuous improvement, customer service, global marketing, new product development, or advanced technology.

Just as being a good project manager and a good communicator are definite assets for career advancement, so is being a good change manager. If you can become more open to change and help reduce resistance of others to change, you will contribute to the development and implementation of new, visible projects. Leaders promote people who help them succeed and who make their jobs easier. As a good change manager, you will be seen as someone whom senior leaders can count on to get the job done—a real plus in today's work environment. In Chapter 1 you identified your desired future. If you learn to plan for change, you are more likely to realize your dream.

The third benefit, increased marketability, is important because everyone likes to have options, especially about where they work. If you have a reputation for being flexible and trying new things, you are a strong candidate for any organization. On the other hand, if you are rigid and too committed to doing things "the old way," it is less likely that an outside firm will gamble on you to fit into their organization. Having personal conviction is fine, but flexibility is much more marketable than rigidity.

Finally, since planned change is always easier than unplanned changed, learning to effectively manage change reduces personal stress (job-related or personal), increases confidence, and enhances opportunities for professional development. All of these lead to increased job satisfaction.

If you manage change effectively, you will probably realize all of the potential benefits listed above: job security, career advancement, improved marketability, and increased job satisfaction. Which, if any, are important to you?

Benefits of Managing Change

Circle which benefits of effective change management are important to you:

    a. Job security

    b. Career advancement

    c. Improved marketability

    d. Increased job satisfaction

Now explore each benefit a little more carefully.

1. **Job security**. First, list three possible changes you may soon face at work. Second, list the adaptation required for each change. Finally, list how each change would be a job saver for you.

Example:

Possible Change	*Adaptation Required*	*Job Saver*
a. New technology	*Learn new computer program*	*New business*
b. Reduce waste	*Develop improved process*	*Increased profits*
c. New service/product	*Innovative thinking*	*New market niche*
d. More responsiveness	*New mindset*	*Satisfied customers*

Possible Change	**Adaptation Required**	**Job Saver**
a.		
b.		
c.		

2. **Career advancement.** Consider a promotion you would like for the near future and then answer two questions:

    • What changes would you have to manage in that position?

- How can you demonstrate *now* that you have the ability to manage such changes?

3. **Improved Marketability.** If you were to write a job resume today, what job experience demonstrates flexibility and creativity (e.g., learning a new process, changing jobs, joining a new task force, taking advanced skill training, working with four different team leaders)?

4. **Increased Job Satisfaction.** Which job satisfaction factors will increase if you manage change better?

    ❏ less stress   ❏ increased productivity
    ❏ better use of time   ❏ enhanced competence
    ❏ improved morale   ❏ more confidence
    ❏ more fun   ❏ more respect from team

Experiment With Open Thinking

Another way that you can enhance change management in your group is to experiment with open thinking yourself. Just for one day, promise yourself that you will explore every crazy idea that comes up. If someone at lunch says jokingly, "Wouldn't it be great to be a fly on the wall," develop that idea. Describe what the room might look like to a creature that small. Talk about what would be dangerous and what would be exhilarating. Seize the opportunity to flex your imagination.

In the same spirit of experimentation, if someone at a team meeting suggests you hire a circus clown to draw attention to a new project, do not

lock the person up. Consider what is good about the idea. Ask questions, elaborate on the details, and discuss possible reactions. Talk about other events that might benefit from the appearance of a clown. Just for that day, explore all suggestions as though they were the best you have ever heard.

Just for one day, encourage a colleague to talk about harebrained ideas that have popped up over the years—ideas about how to get rich, how to get a date, how to get *out* of a date, or how to get relatives to finally go home. Or ask another colleague to talk about all-time great excuses—wiggling out of detention, blaming a sibling for something, explaining a dented fender.

Just for one day, you might encourage a child you know to join with you in your open-minded experiment. Ask the child how to make a toy or a game out of any household object (e.g., a paper-towel roll, bread-wrapper tie, empty coffee can). Don't just listen; follow the child's lead by expanding on ideas, responding with, "Yes, and then we could..." Soon you will realize that open thinking is as natural as child's play. Unfortunately, institutions often discourage playfulness and foster a no-nonsense attitude. Perhaps you can initiate, however slowly, a new attitude toward creativity in your workplace. All it takes is a few people in each organization to sow the seeds of change.

"Necessity may be the mother of invention, but play is certainly the father."

Roger von Oech
A Whack on the Side of the Head

If you experiment just for a day, you may find the practice enjoyable enough to try once a month, or you might decide to try your experiment just for one meeting, opening up to all ideas presented at that time. Pick out a person whom you regard as "a little left of center," someone whom humor consultant David Baum describes as "a few sandwiches short of a picnic." Ask that person to help you stretch your thinking. Remember, "weird," "crazy," and "ridiculous" are all relative terms which could easily be exchanged for "creative," "innovative," and "brilliant," depending upon the observer.

Many creativity consultants recommend breaking routine as a way of keeping your mind stimulated. Occasionally drive a different way to work; try something for lunch that you have never eaten before; rearrange the furniture in your office; sit in a different place at meetings. In essence, *change your point of view, so you may see anew.* As you stimulate your mind and strengthen your open thinking, you will become more comfortable with change.

Two techniques you can use to practice open thinking are seeing similarities and abandoning traditional thinking. Each taps your creative mind and moves you to more innovation and change.

TWO STEPS TO OPEN THINKING

- **look for similarities**
- **abandon traditional thinking**

By making connections between the familiar and unfamiliar, we can often make more sense of something new. One way to see similarities is to practice making comparisons. For instance, upon meeting someone new you might say, "Her handshake instantly cemented our relationship." Comparing the handshake to cement helps us vividly understand the firm, bonding capacity of the handshake. It also stimulates thought about what else the two might have in common. What do you think?

Seeing Similarities

1. A handshake is like cement because they both...

   a.

   b.

   c.

   Your answers may have included:
   - They both take on the shape of the receiver.
   - They both can be soft and mushy, or firm and solid.
   - They both hold things together.
   - They both need a "good mix" to work right.
   - They both are better dry than wet.
   - They both feel better warm.
   - They both can be weakened by cracks.
   - They both can be destroyed by force.

2. Now think of a problem your team is trying to solve and experiment with similarities:

   a. In what ways is your problem like a newborn baby?

   b. If your problem were a monster, what would it look like?

3. Did you generate anything new about your problem using comparison?

You can also practice open thinking by occasionally abandoning traditional thought. While logical, analytical thinking is very important in the evaluative, planning stages of problem solving, it is not very helpful in the idea generation stage. To flex your open thinking, try a different route. Skip over the obvious and even consider the ridiculous. You just might open a new door.

Improvement **TIP**

Avoid the Obvious

1. When you want help getting along with a coworker, whom might you ask?

    _____

    (a ten-year old, the cleaning lady, a coworker)

2. To get a fresh perspective on a work problem, what might you take time out to do?

    _____

    (ride a bike, stand on your head, go to an art museum, read a poem, juggle)

3. To understand your team meetings better, what other team might you observe?

    _____

    (a kindergarten class, a little-league practice, a church-choir rehearsal, an hour at a construction site, a marching band, a jazz ensemble)

4. Think of a problem at work. How do you think the following figures would approach the problem?

    *   Attila the Hun:

    *   Lassie:

    *   Jerry Seinfeld:

RESPONSE TO CHANGE IS INFLUENCED BY
• perceived benefits/costs
• past experience
• self-esteem
• abilities
• support

Talk Positively About Change

Another way to influence openness to change within your team is to make a commitment to talk positively about change in general, and workplace changes in particular. While an individual's response to change is influenced by many factors (e.g., perceived benefits and costs, past experience with change, self-esteem, abilities, and available support), peer response is an important factor.

Both positive and negative attitudes about workplace change can be very contagious. Think of how tempting it is to reinforce a colleague who grumbles, "One more stupid change brought on by the guys upstairs just to drive us crazy." The complainer may be a friend and normally quite reasonable. Perhaps you really want to offer support. But *how* you choose to show support is critical. Letting a colleague vent and communicating that you understand his or her frustration is appropriate and constructive. However, agreeing that the change is stupid, management is incompetent, or that the change will necessarily drive you all crazy is inappropriate and destructive. That type of response will spread resistance to the change and diminish your group's ability to be flexible. A better response would acknowledge the individual's frustration while also acknowledging the need for the change and your confidence in the group's ability to handle it.

How you talk about change in general is also important. If you only talk about the extra work, the confusion, the errors, and the frustration that accompany change, you are reinforcing a notion that change is bad. You should also talk about the excitement, the learning, and the opportunities of change. There is some danger, stress, and discomfort associated with even the most desired changes (e.g., a move to sunny California, a promotion, a new baby, or a marriage). But there is also stimulation, excitement, growth, and opportunity. To be an effective role model for your group, take the risk of talking about the opportunities of change. Help your associates see both sides of change's double-edged sword by reframing situations to focus on the opportunity of change.

Seeing Opportunity in Change

For each change situation below, identify both the *dangers* and the *opportunities* associated with the change.

Situation	Dangers	Opportunities
1. Your team is asked to develop your own budget.		
2. You are asked to represent your team on a task force.		

Check your answers with the example below.

Example:

Situation	Dangers	Opportunities
1. *Your team is asked to develop its own budget*	• *team may fight over priorities* • *must learn new techniques* • *will take too much time*	• *more control over allocations* • *more respect from management* • *learn budgeting techniques to use at home*
2. *You are asked to represent your team on a task force*	• *you might not do a good job* • *you will have to miss an hour a week of TV to prepare*	• *strengthen your presentation skills* • *be more visible to management—more promotable* • *many will respect you for taking the job*

Talk Positively About Change

In the left column list all of the negative terms you hear people use to describe change. In the right column, list as many positive descriptors as you can. Then make a contract with yourself to use more of the positive terms and avoid the negative words or phrases.

Change is... (negative)	Change is... (positive)
• stressful	• exciting
• time consuming	• growth producing
• hard work	• challenging
•	•
•	•
•	•
•	•
•	•
•	•
•	•
•	•
•	•
•	•

What Can Your Team Do To Enhance Change Management?

3 TEAM
IMPROVEMENT
STRATEGIES

Study Human Response to Change

Skill in change management begins with an understanding of how people generally respond to change and what can be done to reduce resistance to change.

Since change represents giving up an old way for a new way, there is always an element of loss. Common fears related to change can be better understood in terms of losses associated with workplace change.

1. Study human response to change.
2. Discuss recent changes.
3. Create an innovative climate.

Common Fears Related to Workplace Change

Fear	*Related Loss*
1. Increased workload ⟶	Loss of comfort
2. The unknown ⟶	Loss of security
3. New people ⟶	Loss of belonging
4. Failure ⟶	Loss of esteem
5. Boredom ⟶	Loss of interest, self-actualization

The five fears and related losses can be associated with what Abraham Maslow described as a hierarchy of human needs. According to Maslow, individuals are generally driven to satisfy these needs in an ascending order. From the bottom up, an increased workload frustrates our comfort or physical needs. Lack of information feeds our fear of the unknown because it jeopardizes our security needs. A change in work teams affects our need to belong, and fear of not succeeding threatens our need to be recognized or to achieve status. Finally, a change in job duties can threaten our need to self-actualize or use all of our talents.

Related Fears

Maslow's Hierarchy of Human Needs

Boredom —————→ Self actualization (using one's talent)

Failure ———→ Recognition (esteem needs)

New people ————→ Belonging (social needs)

The unknown ————→ Security (predictability needs)

Increased workload ——→ Physical (comfort needs)

Fortunately, there are many ways to reduce the resistance which so often accompanies change, and you can learn such strategies as a team. There are many seminars available on this topic; your team might attend one together. Perhaps your internal training department offers such a course or can arrange to have one brought in. The course content should include typical response to change, factors that influence individual response to change, and strategies for decreasing resistance to change. It might also address how to reduce the stress of change, how to help others through change, and how to "freeze" a change once it is operational.

Discuss Recent Changes

At a team meeting, your group can discuss changes that members have survived outside of work. Individuals might discuss their responses to each change—what concerns they had, what helped them through the change, and what could have been done differently. Since this discussion is actually testimony to each individual's ability to survive change, it will foster confidence in the team and increase security. It may also generate a few ideas on how to effectively handle future changes. TEAM ACTIVITY 16: CHANGES YOU'VE SURVIVED*, will assist you in this pursuit.

*Reproducible masters of Team Activity 16 and all other individual and team activities in this book can be found in *50 Activities For Teams At Work*, Suzanne Willis Zoglio, Tower Hill Press, Doylestown, PA.

team activity

16   CHANGES YOU'VE SURVIVED

1. Check any personal changes you have experienced in the past year.

    ❑ marriage   ❑ new social group

    ❑ divorce   ❑ new hobby

    ❑ death in family   ❑ broke old habit

    ❑ new baby   ❑ back to school

    ❑ new home   ❑ health change

2. Which change was the most difficult?

3. What doubts did you have about the change?

4. What helped you cope with the change?

5. What would have helped you better adjust to the change?

You might also discuss workplace changes that team members have survived (new bosses, new equipment, reduced budgets, new regulations). Focus on what doubts were associated with the change and what helped. See TEAM ACTIVITY 17: WORKPLACE CHANGE ANALYSIS.

Create an Innovative Climate

Since behaviors that are positively reinforced are likely to continue, you should make a real effort to support change by discussing new ideas, encouraging risk taking, and recognizing innovation.

---

team activity

17 WORKPLACE CHANGE ANALYSIS

1. Check any workplace changes you have experienced in the past year.

   ❑ different position   ❑ new "rules"
   ❑ new boss   ❑ new responsibility
   ❑ new work group   ❑ new product/service
   ❑ new equipment   ❑ new "customers"

2. Which change was most difficult?

3. What doubts did you have about the change?

4. What helped you cope with the change?

5. What would have helped you better adjust to the change?

Whether you discuss new ideas one-on-one with team members or in a group is not as important as doing it. You probably have a new idea for improving things every day but suppress it because you think that no one will be interested, or that it will take too much work to implement, or that management won't approve. The next time a light bulb flashes on in your head, share it. Discuss all of the reasons it's a great idea *before* you get into any reasons why the idea might not fly. TEAM ACTIVITY 18: IDEAS FOR CHANGE, may help you formulate your thoughts.

team activity

18   IDEAS FOR CHANGE

Complete each item below.

1. What would you like to see changed about your work team?

❏ a procedure	❏ paperwork	❏ meeting format
❏ a measurement	❏ turnaround time	❏ equipment
❏ record keeping	❏ training	❏ cafeteria
❏ celebrations	❏ computer program	❏ newsletter
❏ employee recognition	❏ community involvement	❏ leadership rotation
❏ performance rewards	❏ safety	❏ stress reduction
❏ time management	❏ communication	❏ problem solving
❏ decision making	❏ library	❏ cross-department cooperation

    ❏ other(s):

2. How would you like the items to change?

3. What would be a good opportunity to discuss your idea with your team?

To encourage risk taking, praise people when they go out on a limb. When someone offers a far-out idea, praise the person for their original thinking. When someone takes an unpopular position, praise their courage to "swim upstream." When people risk looking foolish by asking questions, praise their willingness to clarify a point for the team. To see how much your team encourages/discourages risk taking, complete TEAM ACTIVITY 19: RISK-TAKING QUIZ.

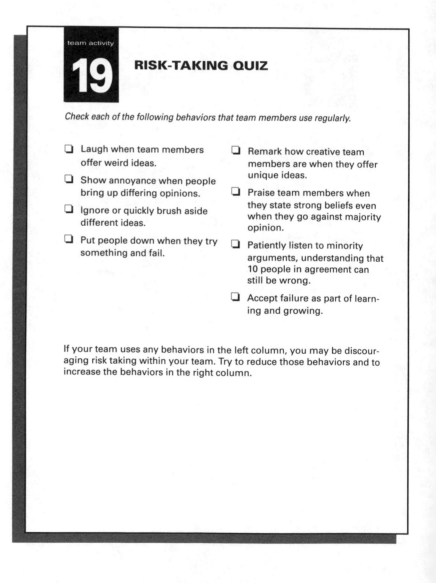

team activity

19   RISK-TAKING QUIZ

Check each of the following behaviors that team members use regularly.

❏ Laugh when team members offer weird ideas.

❏ Show annoyance when people bring up differing opinions.

❏ Ignore or quickly brush aside different ideas.

❏ Put people down when they try something and fail.

❏ Remark how creative team members are when they offer unique ideas.

❏ Praise team members when they state strong beliefs even when they go against majority opinion.

❏ Patiently listen to minority arguments, understanding that 10 people in agreement can still be wrong.

❏ Accept failure as part of learning and growing.

If your team uses any behaviors in the left column, you may be discouraging risk taking within your team. Try to reduce those behaviors and to increase the behaviors in the right column.

You can recognize innovation by publicly acknowledging innovative members. Print their pictures in newsletters, post great ideas on bulletin boards, verbally congratulate people at meetings, and provide feedback on the impact of innovation (e.g., dollars saved, customers gained, accidents avoided). TEAM ACTIVITY 20: RECOGNIZING INNOVATION, might help you think of ways to recognize innovative team members. When you create an innovative team climate, you encourage effective change management by increasing the potential rewards of peer approval and recognition.

team activity

RECOGNIZING INNOVATION

Check the following recognition ideas that you could implement in your group.

❑ Great idea bulletin board
❑ Team meeting "toast" to innovators
❑ Newsletter "light bulb" column; naming the "Edison" of your team
❑ Free lunch coupons for innovators
❑ Special parking for innovator of the month
❑ Comedy video collection—lend an idea, borrow a video
❑ Other:

❑ Other:

❑ Other:

CHAPTER 6

SUMMARY

- Teams need to manage change if they are to keep up with advances in technology, fluctuations in the economy, expansion of competition, changes in customer demands, and shifts in employee expectations.

- Teams that manage change well are better problem solvers, higher risk takers, and more open thinkers. Members see change as an opportunity more than as a danger and frequently seek ways to change.

- Members can enhance change management by identifying the personal benefits, experimenting with open thinking, and talking positively about change.

- Teams can enhance change management by studying human response to change, discussing recent changes, and creating a climate for innovation.

CHAPTER

"Toto, I have a feeling we're not in Kansas anymore."

Dorothy
The Wizard of Oz

CONNECTIONS

In today's organizations, gone are the days of the solo performer. Teams must connect their work with the goals of the larger organization, collaborate with each other, and work with other units to enhance their performance and develop a positive work climate.

In hospitals, physicians must work with nurses, and nurses with pharmacists. House-keeping must work with dietary, and dietary must work with volunteer services. To deliver high-quality patient care, hospital teams must connect flawlessly. It is the only way to provide seamless care for patients, improve processes, and contain costs.

In public schools, board members must join forces with administrators to find educationally appropriate ways of dealing with fiscal restraints. Administrators must join forces with teachers to work out mutually acceptable ways of inspiring children to lifelong learning. Teachers must join with community members to share expertise and support innovative approaches. To prepare our youth for the challenges of tomorrow, taxpayers, board members, administrators, teachers, and community members must forge relationships and be driven by the mission they share: To educate our youth.

In business organizations, sales must work well with production, and production with customer service. Human resources must coordinate with legal, and legal must coordinate with finance. If turf wars surface and employees practice compartmental thinking, high performance is impossible. Only work groups which remain flexible, responsive, and well connected are able to move ideas, projects, and products successfully through a system.

To compete effectively, organizations must fashion a network of employees who support each other as they support organizational priorities. Every team needs strong connections to accomplish its mission. Nurturing such connections is as necessary as learning technical skills.

How to Recognize a Team With Strong Connections

There are three types of connections important to a work team: connection to the organization as a whole, connection to team members, and connection to various groups with whom the team interfaces.

When a work team is connected to the organization as a whole, members discuss team performance in relationship to corporate priorities, customer feedback, and quality measures. They demonstrate an interest in how their organization is doing overall and how they can contribute to overall success.

If team members have established strong connections with each other, peer support manifests in subtle ways. Colleagues volunteer help without being asked, cover for each other in a

THREE IMPORTANT CONNECTIONS

- **to organization**
- **to team members**
- **to other teams**

pinch, congratulate each other publicly, share resources, offer constructive criticism, find ways to socialize, and celebrate together.

Team members who maintain good relations with individuals outside of their team typically perceive coworkers from other areas as their "internal customers." They routinely ask their internal customers for feedback on how they can serve them better. They treat requests of their internal customers with the same respect that they show an external customer's requests. They engage in joint problem solving to negotiate any differences. Such collaborative work groups also exchange ideas for improvement and share resources such as training films, books, and videos.

In a work group with strong connections there are more interdepartmental meetings and more informal get-togethers. Well-connected groups tend to communicate and play together more frequently than isolated teams. Team members often eat lunch with people from other areas and sit with non-team members at social events.

If a team has developed solid connections, there is little blaming or grumbling by team members that senior management or other groups are blocking team productivity. There is more sensitivity to the needs of other groups and more sharing of credit for daily successes. All of these are signs that a work group has successfully moved from a stage of dependence (where members blame others for their failure or success) through independence (where members take responsibility for results) to interdependence (where members collaborate with other groups for win/win results).

THREE TEAM STAGES
- **dependence**
- **independence**
- **interdependence**

What Can You Do To Enhance Connections?

INDIVIDUAL IMPROVEMENT STRATEGIES

1. Encourage a big-picture focus.
2. Strengthen relationships within your team.
3. Develop relation-ships with other teams.
4. Volunteer for interdepartmental projects.

Encourage a Big-Picture Focus

Since commitment to organizational priorities and relationships with other work groups can be advanced or set back by individual team members, there are numerous things you can person-ally do to enhance your group's connections. If your company's mission, values, and goals are published, post them in your work area along with company-wide performance results and suc-cesses. In addition, whenever your group explores a decision, refer to the overall corporate objectives to see if the solutions you are consid-ering are in alignment with organizational priori-ties. If you have questions regarding a "big pic-ture" issue, suggest that your group invite a senior manager in to a team meeting to discuss the issues. Right now, examine how connections make the whole organization work.

How Connections Make Things Work

1. What are your organization's priority goals for the next year?

2. How will your team contribute to the achievement of those goals?

3. For your team to perform its best, what do you need from other departments/teams?

   a.

   b.

   c.

   d.

4. What do those teams need from you?

   a.

   b.

   c.

   d.

Strengthen Relationships Within Your Team

Connecting with your team members goes beyond keeping your commitments, communicating, and managing conflict. For strong connections, you need to develop trust by getting to know individuals, showing respect for their opinions, valuing their diversity, and recognizing their contributions. Powerful personal connections are made (or diminished) one interaction at a time. Sometimes the smallest gestures—a birthday card, a public apology, an inquiry about a sick relative, an offer to help, an invitation to lunch, a shared concern—have the biggest impact on team relationships.

Improvement
TIP

Develop Relationships
With Other Teams

This strategy may sound overly simple, but just stop for a minute. Think of a department with which you interface. Now try to describe an average day in the life of someone in that department. What do they face when they arrive at work? What equipment do they need to master? What kinds of crises do they deal with? How do they measure their productivity? What are their priority goals this year? How many other groups do they interact with daily? How many suppliers do they deal with? How many different customers do they serve? How are they recognized for contributions to the organization? What successes have they recently experienced? What changes have they faced recently? The answers do not come that quickly, do they? It is very easy to get wrapped up in our own area and fail to take interest in other work groups. How can you find out more about other groups in order to enhance your connections with them?

One way is to take different paths when you come into work, go to lunch, or leave at night. Intentionally walk by, or even *through*, another department. Stop briefly to observe, ask questions, and exchange pleasantries. It is truly amazing how such a small change can impact your relationships with others. It will also add interest to your work day as you break with routine.

Job swapping for a day is another way of learning about other work environments. Many organizations encourage associates from one department to "job shadow" in another department for a day. You might consider one such adventure every three months. There is nothing like being in the trenches to really understand what gunfire sounds like. And there is nothing more credible than being able to say, "I've been there. I know what you mean."

You can also read literature and corporate newsletter articles from other departments. It is interesting how many people scan such information only to see if it pertains to them directly. If not, they pass over the information. Set a goal for yourself to regularly read about the work groups with whom you interface. Scan department brochures, articles in your company newsletter, and their product information. Focus on what you can learn about the department's needs, priorities, and values. Try to learn what challenges they face, how they contribute to overall customer satisfaction, and how they might perceive your work group.

It's difficult to meet expectations of a group if you don't understand their needs, but it's even more difficult to ask for support from others if you don't meet their expectations. Consider one department or team you could interface with more effectively. How well do you know them?

Improvement TIP

THREE STEPS TO BETTER CONNECTIONS

- **understand the needs of others**
- **try to meet their expectations**
- **ask for support**

Partnership Interview

Team/Department:

Names of team members:

-

-

-

-

Leader:

Basic purpose:

Equipment they use:

Expertise necessary:

Primary customers:

Things that block performance:

Things that facilitate performance:

Comments:

By developing positive relationships with other teams, you increase your chances for collaborative efforts between your team and theirs. Long-standing, open communications and reciprocal support lead to the kind of trust that is necessary for negotiating across department lines. If the only contact between work teams is when there is a problem, then the resolution will be slow at best, and impossible at worst. By being open to people outside of your team—eating lunch with others, car-pooling with others—you can actually strengthen connections for your work group.

Volunteer for Interdepartmental Projects

Every time you work on an interdepartmental team, you create an opportunity to help others understand what your group does and what it needs. You also increase your understanding of what other work groups do and need. In addition, you may learn how to communicate more effectively by picking up terminology that is common to one group but foreign to you and your group. If you are a good observer of human behavior, you might determine a few personal style differences: Which individuals are persuaded by details and facts? Which seem to make decisions from instinct? Which colleagues are driven by a broad sense of purpose? Which people need day-to-day plans?

The more you learn about others, the better you will be able to communicate *and* negotiate. Also, the more you allow others to get to know you, the more comfortable they will be in collaborating with you and your team. People who work together on projects often develop strong bonds and are more willing to trust each other.

What Can Your Team Do To Enhance Connections?

4 TEAM IMPROVEMENT STRATEGIES

1. Stay in touch with management.

2. Get involved with corporate-wide issues.

3. Foster team interactions

4. Support other teams.

Stay in Touch With Management

Occasionally invite management visitors to team meetings to discuss organizational goals, performance data, and profitability indicators. Ask how your team can contribute, and offer suggestions for immediate actions. Hold regular (bimonthly or quarterly) management/team liaison meetings to iron out any concerns, make your resource needs clear, and communicate your team's successes. Prior to a meeting you might use questions similar to those found in TEAM ACTIVITY 21: IN TOUCH WITH MANAGEMENT*, to survey senior management regarding new corporate priorities, particularly trouble spots or areas where your group might be able to help. Then, as a team, you can brainstorm ways that you can contribute more to organizational success. Once you have identified strategies for enhancing team contribution, write a summary of proposed initiatives to communicate your awareness of corporate priorities and your interest in making a difference.

---

*Reproducible masters of Team Activity 21 and all other individual and team activities in this book can be found in *50 Activities For Teams At Work*, Suzanne Willis Zoglio, Tower Hill Press, Doylestown, PA.

team activity

21 IN TOUCH WITH MANAGEMENT

Consider the following questions as you develop your understanding of the connections between your team and management.

1. What does management want to see improved over the next six months?

2. What are the biggest "headaches" for management right now?

3. How would management like your group to help?

4. How many of your team's recent accomplishments have been communicated to management?

5. How many things on your team's "wish list" (e.g., equipment, training, scheduling, policy revision) have been formally requested from management?

Get Involved With Corporate-Wide Issues

Your team can volunteer to maintain a "public" area such as an employee garden, lobby, lunchroom, or snack area or take your turn on the customer hotline. You can also sort through a week's worth of consumer mail, rotate through the reception area as a company ambassador, or submit articles to the company newsletter. You might even suggest that representatives job shadow a senior executive or two to enhance your group's understanding of big-picture concerns. Brainstorm ways your team can get involved at the corporate level, using ideas in TEAM ACTIVITY 22: OUTREACH IDEAS, as a springboard for your own ideas.

Improvement
TIP

22 OUTREACH IDEAS

To generate ideas for strengthening connections by getting involved with organization-wide concerns, spend 15 minutes at your next team meeting brainstorming ideas for these categories.

1. What community cause might you spearhead as an interdepartmental project?
   Example: Collecting clothing/supplies for the homeless.

2. What common area could you "spruce up" to contribute something to your company team?
   Example: Take responsibility for acquiring and rotating employee art for the dining room.

3. What writing projects would connect you to the rest of the organization?
   Example: Start an employee poetry journal.

4. Others?

Foster Team Interactions

It is important for a team to continually address cohesiveness among its members. Opportunities for connecting one-on-one should be encouraged and orchestrated regularly. You might end staff meetings 15 minutes early to socialize, schedule monthly lunches, create team projects, circulate member profiles, or ask one member a month to provide feedback on what specific support he or she received from a team member and what additional support would be appreciated.

Teams can also strengthen connections within the team by "sanctioning" talk about life outside of work and about individual work styles. You might try posting a blank graffiti sheet similar to that shown in TEAM ACTIVITY 23: TEAM GRAFFITI,

---

TO FOSTER COHESIVENESS

- socialize at meetings
- schedule team lunches
- create team projects
- circulate member profiles
- provide feedback

team activity

23 TEAM GRAFFITI

Ask each team member to sign and fill in the columns.

Name	A job I once had....	On Saturdays I like to...	I really appreciate coworkers who...
1.			
2.			
3.			
4.			
5.			
6.			
7.			
8.			
9.			
10.			

before your next meeting. Ask everyone to contribute during a coffee break and then review the components at the close of your meeting.

Support Other Teams

To enhance your team's connections with other work groups, try scheduling monthly cross-departmental meetings with a different department each month. If you have an official work team leader, be sure that he or she is developing a strong relationship with leaders of other work groups. Leaders can often make or break cooperation between groups.

Improvement
TIP

If you hear of a personnel crunch in another department (due to the flu, turnover, unusual workload, etc.) discuss how your team might help out. For instance, you might "loan" a team member for a day, cover telephones at lunch, or temporarily take responsibility for one of the group's company-wide tasks (e.g., arranging seminars, booking speakers, or organizing the company picnic).

Once your group focuses on ways of supporting other departments, you will be surprised at how many ideas you generate. And when you start strengthening your relationships with other groups, you will be amazed at how much support comes *back* to your team. Use TEAM ACTIVITY 24: KEEPING COMMUNICATIONS OPEN, to develop ways of keeping interdepartmental communications open.

Building connections is like buying insurance—you don't use it every day, but when you need it, you are mighty glad you paid the premium.

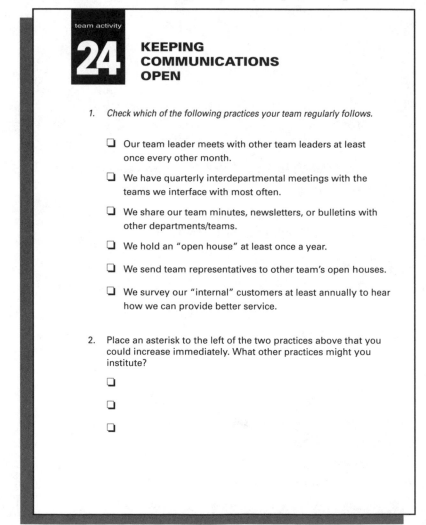

team activity

24 KEEPING COMMUNICATIONS OPEN

1. *Check which of the following practices your team regularly follows.*

   ❏ Our team leader meets with other team leaders at least once every other month.

   ❏ We have quarterly interdepartmental meetings with the teams we interface with most often.

   ❏ We share our team minutes, newsletters, or bulletins with other departments/teams.

   ❏ We hold an "open house" at least once a year.

   ❏ We send team representatives to other team's open houses.

   ❏ We survey our "internal" customers at least annually to hear how we can provide better service.

2. Place an asterisk to the left of the two practices above that you could increase immediately. What other practices might you institute?

   ❏

   ❏

   ❏

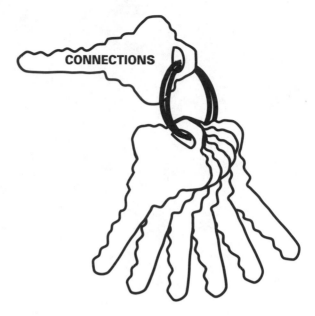

CONNECTIONS

CHAPTER 7
SUMMARY

- Three important connections for work teams are: connection to the large organization and its goals, connection to team members, and connection to other teams (e.g., internal customers, suppliers, or neighbors).

- Members can enhance team connections by encouraging a big-picture focus, strengthening relationships with team members, developing relationships with other teams, and volunteering for interdepartmental projects.

- Teams can enhance connections by staying in touch with management, getting involved with corporate-wide issues, fostering team interactions, and supporting other teams.

SELECTED READINGS

Beckhard, R., and Pritchard, W. *Changing the Essence*. San Francisco: Jossey-Bass, 1992.

Block, Peter. *The Empowered Manager: Positive Political Skills at Work*. San Francisco: Jossey-Bass, 1987.

Covey, Stephen. *Seven Habits of Highly Effective People*. New York: Simon and Schuster, 1989.

DePree, M. *Leadership is an Art*. New York: Dell Publishing, 1989.

DePree, M. *Leadership Jazz*. New York: Doubleday, 1992.

Fisher, R., and Ury, W. *Getting to Yes*. New York: Penguin Books, 1991.

Goodman, Paul A., and Associates. *Designing Effective Work Groups*. San Francisco: Jossey-Bass, 1990.

Hackman, J. Richard, ed. *Groups That Work (And Those That Don't)*. San Francisco: Jossey-Bass, 1986.

Kanter, R. M. *The Change Masters*. New York: Simon and Schuster, 1983.

Peters, Tom. *Thriving on Chaos: Handbook for a Management Revolution*. New York: Alfred A. Knopf, 1987.

Peters, Thomas J., and Waterman, Robert H. Jr. *In Search of Excellence*. New York: Harper & Row, 1982.

Pfeiffer, J. William, and Jones, John. *A Handbook of Structured Experiences for Human Relations Training*, Vol. III. La Jolla: University Associates, 1974.

Scholtes, Peter. *The Team Handbook*. Madison: Joiner Associates, 1988.

Senge, Peter M. *The Fifth Discipline*. New York: Doubleday Currency, 1990.

Smith, Douglas K., and Katzenbach, Jon R. *The Wisdom of Teams*. Boston: Harvard Business School Press, 1993.

Ury, William. *Getting Past No*. New York: Bantam Books, 1991.

von Oech, R. *A Whack on the Side of the Head*. New York: Warner Books, Inc., 1983.

Waterman, Robert H. Jr. *The Renewal Factor*. New York: Bantam Books, 1988.

Waterman, Robert H. Jr. *Adhocracy: The Power To Change*. Knoxville, TN: Whittle, 1990.

Weisbord, Marvin R. *Productive Workplaces: Organizing & Managing for Dignity, Meaning & Community*. San Francisco: Jossey-Bass, 1987.

AVAILABLE SUPPORT MATERIALS

50 Activities for Teams At Work

This set contains all of the team activities included in *Teams At Work: 7 Keys To Success*. A facilitator's instruction sheet and reproducible handout is included for each of the 25 individual activities and 25 team activities.

Leader's Guide for Teams At Work: 7 Keys To Success

This loose-leaf guide contains: leader's notes and lesson plans for mini sessions, *50 Activities for Teams At Work*, suggested readings, and tips on reinforcing learning between sessions.

Order these materials through your book and training materials distributor or through Tower Hill Press at 215-345-1338.